IMAGES
of America

ALONG THE
COOPER RIVER
CAMDEN TO HADDONFIELD

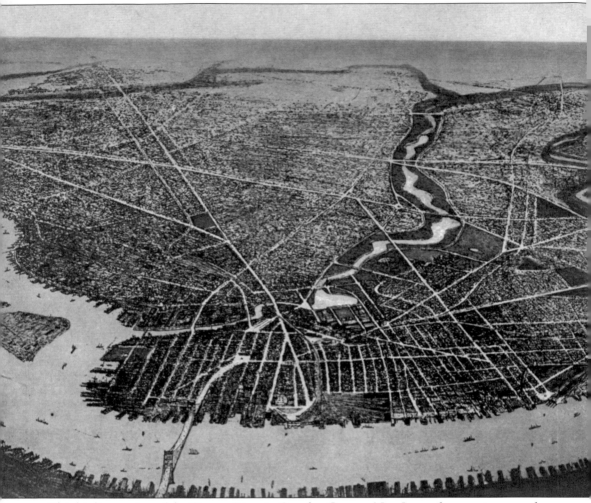

This bird's-eye view of the Cooper River in Camden County, New Jersey, faces east, as seen from above Philadelphia. (Image from *Health, Sunshine and Wealth* [see bibliography].)

ON THE COVER: The Evans Mill on Cooper's Creek at the end of Old Bortons Mill Road in Cherry Hill was the last of a series of water-powered mills dating to Kendall's Free Lodge Mill, built near this location in 1697. Mills were central to the agricultural economy of West Jersey for 200 years. The mill closed in 1897, and fire destroyed it in 1913. Nothing remains at the site. (Courtesy of the Camden County Historical Society.)

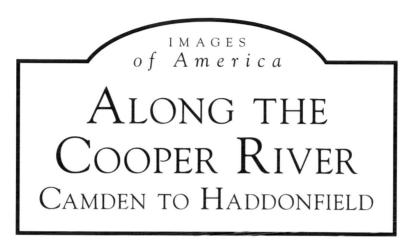

IMAGES
of America

ALONG THE
COOPER RIVER
CAMDEN TO HADDONFIELD

Robert A. Shinn and Kevin Cook
with the Camden County Historical Society

ARCADIA
PUBLISHING

Copyright © 2014 by Robert A. Shinn and Kevin Cook with the Camden County Historical
    Society
ISBN 978-1-4671-2269-6

Published by Arcadia Publishing
Charleston, South Carolina

Printed in the United States of America

Library of Congress Control Number: 2014941801

For all general information, please contact Arcadia Publishing:
Telephone 843-853-2070
Fax 843-853-0044
E-mail sales@arcadiapublishing.com
For customer service and orders:
Toll-Free 1-888-313-2665

Visit us on the Internet at www.arcadiapublishing.com

To Roxane Shinn, who assisted and encouraged us along the way.

CONTENTS

Acknowledgments   6

Introduction   7

1.   The Original People and Cooper's Ferry   9

2.   Haddonfield   19

3.   Camden Industry   37

4.   Ferries and the Delaware River Bridge   49

5.   Recreation along the Cooper River   59

6.   Bridges, Boulevard, and Airport   75

7.   The Parkway Plan and Munn's Meadow Park   87

8.   Pennypacker Park and the Civilian Conservation Corps   99

9.   The Works Progress Administration Builds
      Cooper River Lake   107

10.   Cooper River Park   117

Bibliography   127

ACKNOWLEDGMENTS

We thank the Camden County Historical Society board of trustees, president Chris Perks, director Jason Allen, and library and research director Jacinda Williams for their help. The society maintains a unique research library for genealogical and historical research, the Camden County Museum of History, and Pomona Hall (the 18th-century home of Camden's Cooper family).

We are grateful to Sandra Turner-Barnes, the executive director of the Camden County Cultural and Heritage Commission at Camden County College, and Barbara Laynor, Camden County College Library director, for access to county and park photographs and historical documents.

Our special thanks goes to Paul W. Schopp, consultant historian, for generously sharing his extensive collection of postcards and photographs and his encyclopedic knowledge of Camden County history.

We are grateful to the Historical Society of Haddonfield (HSH) and librarian Katherine Tassinni for permission to publish the society's images, and to volunteer photographer Cliff Brunker for access to HSH and other images.

Our gratitude also goes to the following individuals who gave valuable advice and helped find or granted use of images: Dennis Raible, Sandra Greer White, William Brahms, Mark Zeigler, Rich Magee and the West Jersey Chapter of the National Railroad Historic Society, Richard Weldon, Robert Fisher-Hughes, James Orefice, Louise K. Cook, Margaret Westfield, Brian Kelly, Kevin Kirsche, Mark Barone, and Linda Barniskis.

The names and initials of the individuals and institutions who provided images for this publication include the Camden County Historical Society (CCHS); Paul Schopp (PS); the Historical Society of Haddonfield (HSH); the Camden County Cultural and Heritage Commission at Camden County College (CCC&HC); the Special Collections Research Center, Temple University Libraries, Philadelphia, Pennsylvania, (SCRCTUL); the Camden County Park Commission (CCPC); the Library Company of Philadelphia (LCP); the Independence Seaport Museum (ISM); the William G. Rohrer Memorial Library of the Camden County Library System (CCLS); the Haddonfield Public Library (HPL); Cliff Brunker (CB); Dennis Raible (DR); Robert Shinn (RS); the Cherry Hill Historic Commission (CHHC); the Library of Congress (LOC); the Johnson Victrola Museum (JVM); and Rich Magee and the West Jersey Chapter of the National Railroad Historic Society (WJCNRHS). We credit specific providers by publishing their initials adjacent to the image or image caption. We also credit some images sourced from a Camden County Park Commission (CCPC) publication edited by C. Oscar Brown and a folio assembled by Charles W. Leavitt & Son titled *Health, Sunshine and Wealth* (HSW). We include both references in the bibliography.

INTRODUCTION

Along the Delaware River in the late 17th century, settlers relied on rivers and creeks for survival as there were few roads. English Quakers built homes along Cooper's Creek from its confluence with the Delaware River to Haddonfield, the limit of the creek's upstream tidal reach, and used the tide to transport products in flatboats and scows to and from Philadelphia.

William Cooper was one of the first Quakers to settle along the waterway the English called Deer Creek. After Cooper acquired a 300-acre plantation in 1681 where the creek joins the Delaware River and for the next 230 years, the creek's name appeared on maps as Cooper's Creek. Because federal funds were only available to dredge "rivers," the New Jersey Legislature changed the creek's name in 1911 to Cooper River to increase the county's chances of getting aid to dredge the creek's lower end in Camden.

Prior the 1680, dense forests shaded streams flowing into Cooper's Creek and provided a natural filter to clean its water. By the late 18th century, farmers had cleared vast amounts of creek woodland for firewood and had cut down forests for agriculture. Their plows loosened the soil, causing it to wash down and fill the channels of the many streams flowing into the creek.

The Cooper River is 16 miles long. Its South Branch starts in Gibbsboro, 202 feet above sea level. There are 57 miles of watercourse along the Cooper's branches and its tributaries, draining a 40-square-mile watershed. The North and South Branches have a combined average water flow of 35 million gallons per day.

Today, 70 percent of the land in the Cooper River Watershed is developed. Soil erosion and sedimentation of the Cooper River has worsened as uncontrolled storm-water runoff, nonpoint pollution, and residual pollutants in sediment continue to threaten the river's water quality.

Until a tidal gate was constructed across the Cooper River east of Kaighn Avenue in 1940, the river was navigable from the Delaware River to Grove Street in Haddonfield. Camden County controls tidal flows east of the Kaighn Avenue Tidal Gate to provide storm-water retention capacity and flood control downstream.

Arcadia's Images of America series gives local authors an opportunity to tell the story of their area in pictures. The book's images trace the migration of wealth and power from Camden to its suburbs, showing the best and worst of riverside development. *Along the Cooper River: Camden to Haddonfield* opens a window on the resilience and power of a river to withstand abuse and, despite continuing challenges, start the road to recovery.

One

THE ORIGINAL PEOPLE AND COOPER'S FERRY

The Lenni Lenape, whose name means "original people," settled in the Middle Atlantic region between 1300 and 1400 A.D. Unlike the Europeans who began exploring and trading and then settling to exploit the land and resources along the Delaware River after 1600, the Lenape sustained themselves by growing corns, beans, and squash and hunting fish and game along waterways and springs.

In the 1600s, wars with their Iroquois neighbors to the north and the Susquehannock (Minqua) to the west over control of the fur trade with Europeans, combined with contagious diseases brought by Europeans, decimated the Lenape's numbers. The precipitous decline of their population and competing understandings of what land ownership meant allowed English Quaker settlers to quickly and cheaply "acquire" most of the land in West Jersey between Trenton and Newton Creek beginning in 1677.

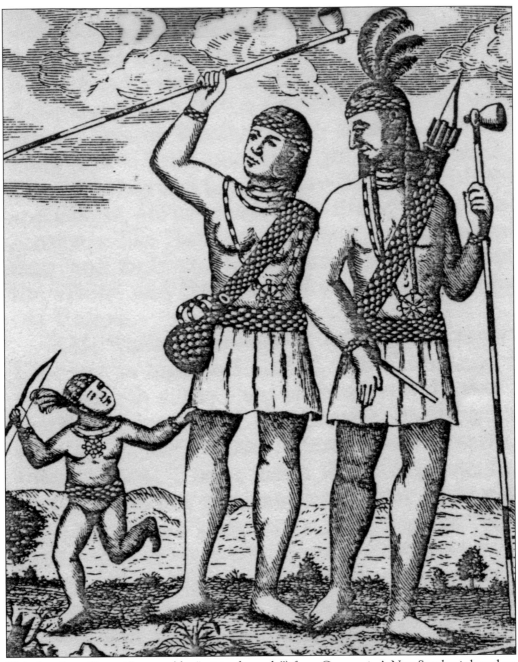

This drawing of Lenni Lenape (the "original people") from Campanius's *New Sweden* is based on a description by Swedish governor Johan Printz's chaplain, who went to America in 1631. War with other tribes, and diseases brought by Europeans, had greatly reduced the numbers of Lenni Lenape by the time William Penn, William Cooper, and waves of other English Quakers arrived to begin buying their land in the 1680s. (CCC&HC.)

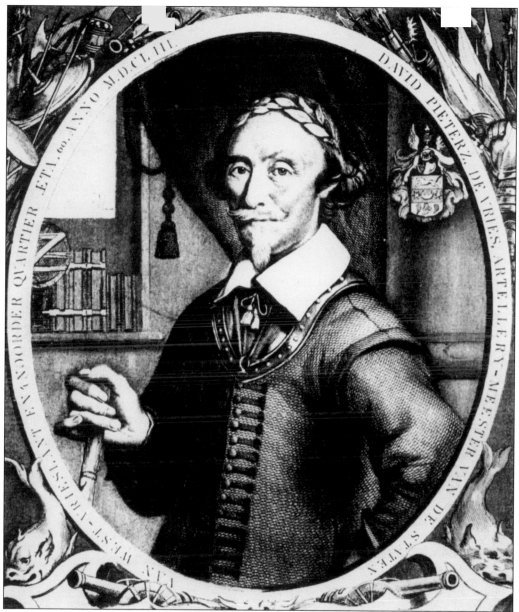

Dutch navigator David Pietersz de Vries was the first European to sail up the Cooper River when he made a return trip to the Delaware River in 1632 and found only the bones of the 34 colonists he had left at the Dutch Fort Nassau the year before. Because he needed to trade for food, de Vries took no revenge. The Lenni Lenape then decoyed de Vries to Timmerkill (Cooper's Creek), where they said the food was stored. De Vries sailed up the creek and anchored near Red Hill (the bluff overlooking Camden's Baird Boulevard Bridge today). That night, a young Lenni Lenape mother, hearing that the men of her tribe planned to slay the Dutch when they landed the next day, paddled a canoe to de Vries's vessel and informed him of the plot. De Vries made his escape and soon after sailed out of the Delaware, abandoning his efforts to colonize New Jersey. (CCC&HC.)

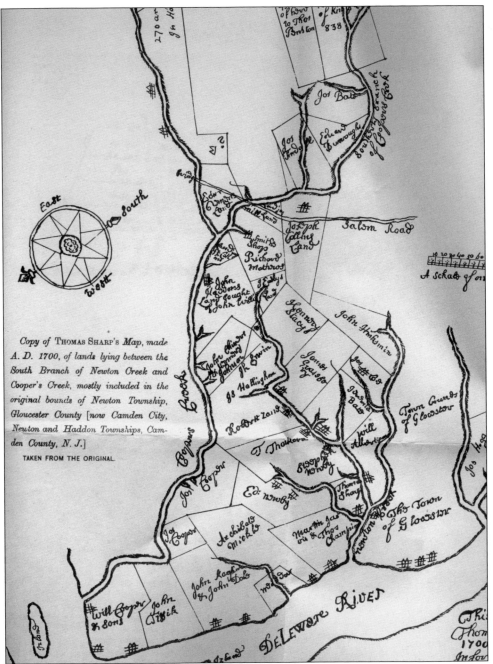

Thomas Sharp's 1700 map shows landholdings between Cooper's and Newton Creeks from the Delaware River to Haddonfield. The names of William Cooper & Sons and Joseph Cooper are on three of the first four large holdings on the south bank of Cooper's Creek from its confluence with the Delaware (bottom left). John Haddon's land is shown farther upstream, south of where the creek's north and south branches join (near the center of the map). The "house" symbol shows the location of Elizabeth Haddon's first log cabin home on this parcel. The Salem Road is shown crossing the North Branch over a bridge, then fording the South Branch north of Buckmans Run at a millpond. (CCHS.)

12

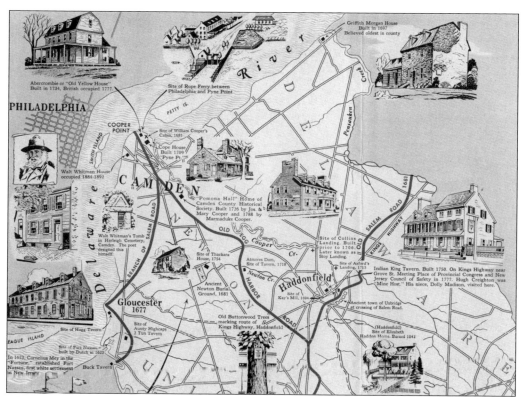

The general locations and appearance of historic buildings and sites along the Cooper River, including the Abercrombie ("Old Yellow House"), the sites of the ferry between Philadelphia and Pyne Point, the site of William Cooper's cabin, the Cope House, Pomona Hall, Walt Whitman's tomb, Collins (later Stoy's) Landing, Axford Landing, the Indian King Tavern, the Elizabeth Haddon (Estaugh) home, and the Kay/Evans Mill are shown on this map. (SCRCTUL.)

Benjamin Cooper, grandson of William Cooper, built this two-and-a-half-story gambrel-roofed stone house at Point and Erie Streets in 1734. When the British army occupied Philadelphia in 1777–1778, the commander of its New Jersey outpost, Lt. Col. Robert Abercrombie, made it his headquarters. The structure may contain part of William Cooper's first house. (CCHS.)

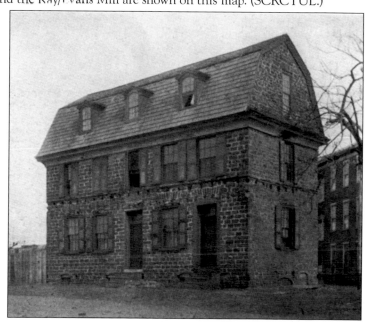

13

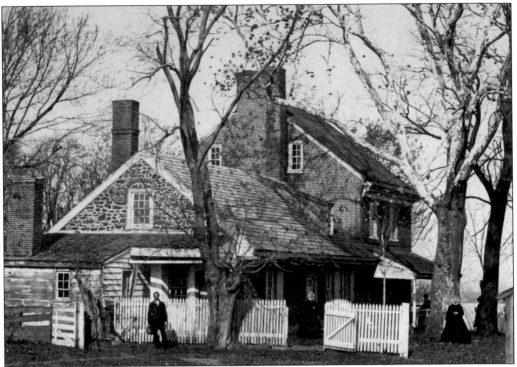

William Cooper built a house above the Delaware River and named it Pyne Poynt for the tall pine forest that grew there. William gave son Joseph a Dutch-style, one-story house (shown on the left side), built in 1695. Also known as the Cope House, it was the oldest extant structure in Camden prior to a 2005 fire. Benjamin Franklin camped near this site in 1723 on his maiden voyage to Philadelphia. (CCHS.)

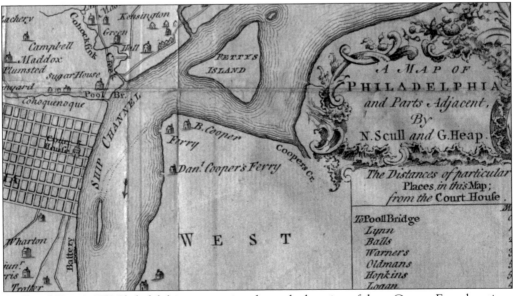

Scull and Heap's 1751 Philadelphia map section shows the location of three Cooper Ferry locations opposite Philadelphia and south of Petty's Island near the mouth of Cooper's Creek. (CCHS.)

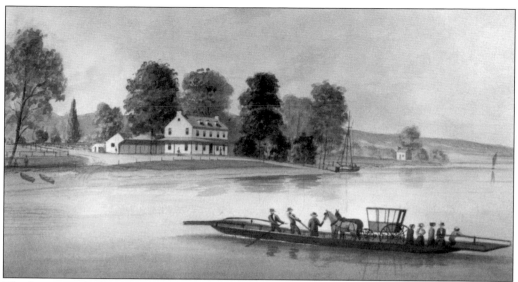

The long-oared wherry carried people, horses, and carriages across the Delaware River. Early Quaker settlers took turns crossing the river on alternate months to attend the monthly meeting at William Cooper's Pyne Poynt home and Thomas Fairman's Shackamaxon house until Philadelphia's meetinghouse was built. William Penn used Fairman's house as his colony's first capitol and, with Cooper and Fairman present, made his first famous treaty with the Indians there. (CCHS.)

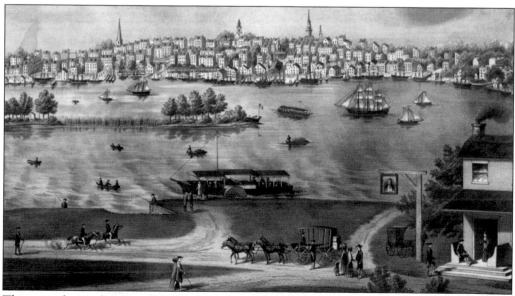

This partial reproduction of F.J. Wade's lithograph *Philadelphia in the Olden Time* shows a horse-powered ferry landing on the Cooper Ferry (Camden) side of the Delaware River, while another ferry rounds Windmill Island. (LOC.)

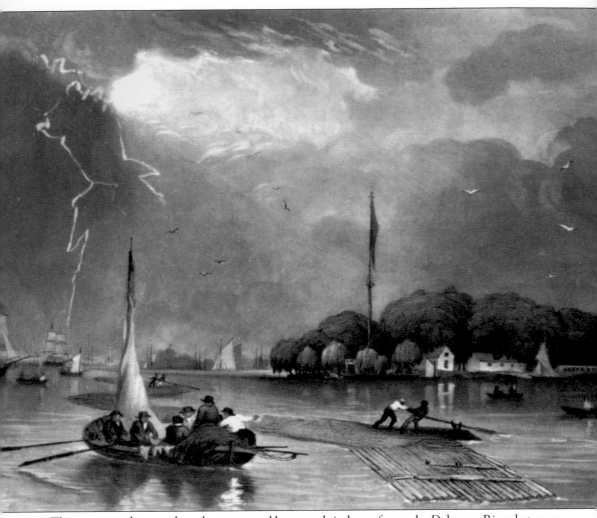

This painting shows sail- and oar-powered boats and timber rafts on the Delaware River between Windmill Island and Philadelphia. Timber cut along the Cooper River was also shipped to Philadelphia by these means. (FLP.)

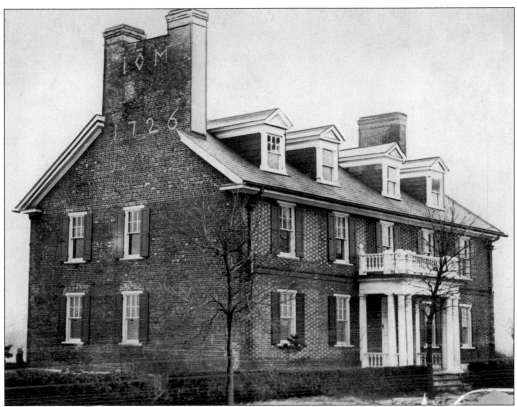

Joseph Cooper Jr., grandson of William Cooper, a leader in the Colonial assembly, and a fruit-tree cultivator, first built on this site after 1713. His youngest brother, Isaac, and then Isaac's son Marmaduke, inherited the plantation. In 1788, Marmaduke transformed a Quaker-style building he inherited into the classic Georgian double-pile mansion with balanced fenestration called Pomona Hall (seen here in 1925). Marmaduke refused to follow the decision of West Jersey Quakers to free their slaves. As a result, he was banned from attending Quaker meetings. Pomona Hall is the current site of the Camden County Historical Society. (SCRCTUL.)

This map shows Cooper's Creek (left of center) and an early network of dirt roads and paths through what became Camden. The Burlington Road runs vertically on the map, crossing the Cooper at Spicer's Ferry. The Road to Haddonfield (running horizontally on the map) originates at each of the three ferry landings shown on the Delaware and ends in Haddonfield, "six and 3/4" miles away. (CCHS.)

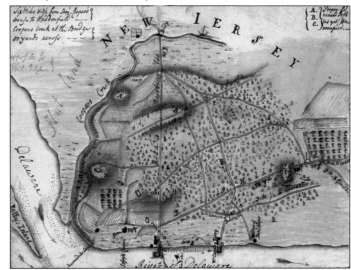

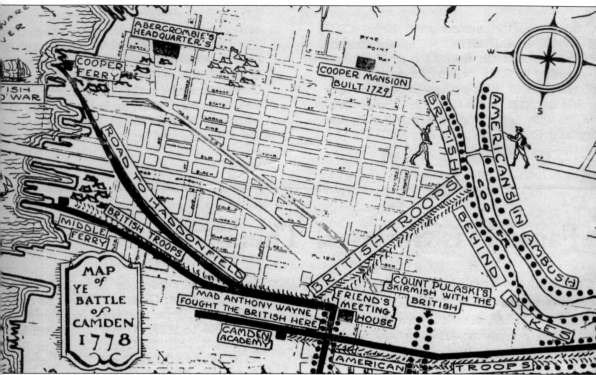

Revolutionary War skirmishes were fought in Camden. In early 1778, the British army was attacked at Cooper's Ferry by American general "Mad" Anthony Wayne and Polish count Casimir Pulaski, the commander of the American cavalry. Gen. George Washington, encamped at Valley Forge after losing Philadelphia, ordered Wayne to disrupt British foraging in South Jersey and to burn the bridge near today's Federal Street to discourage future depredations. The positions of troops along Cooper's Creek and the southern edge of Camden are superimposed on a city street map. The Americans drove the British back to Philadelphia, but they could not occupy Cooper's Ferry, because they would be within range of British warship cannons. (CCHS.)

Two

HADDONFIELD

Settlers and tradesmen were attracted to the Haddonfield area after 1721 when John Haddon gave land for a new Quaker meetinghouse and cemetery. Haddonfield also had other advantages. First, it was located on high ground. Second, it was adjacent to tidal Cooper's Creek, the major transportation highway between Philadelphia, the Delaware River, and the interior of New Jersey until major roads were built years later. Third, it was located on the Old Salem Road between Burlington and Salem, the two major Quaker towns in West Jersey, near a Cooper's Creek ford. Fourth, and perhaps most importantly, the land was owned by a family dedicated to subdividing its large holdings and selling or renting town plots to tradesmen with skills essential to supporting and providing services to the surrounding farmers.

Having developed into a substantial Colonial village of 40 buildings during the American Revolution, Haddonfield regularly hosted the officers and men of the British and American armies as the British sought to consolidate their capture of Philadelphia in 1777 and each sought to obtain for itself, and block the other from, South Jersey's agricultural bounty during the British occupation.

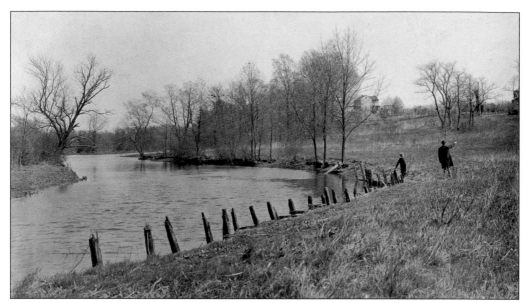

In this 1909 photograph, Samuel Nicholson Rhodes shows son Evan where Elizabeth Haddon lived after arriving from England in 1701. Elizabeth married Quaker minister John Estaugh in 1702 and lived with him in a house on the south bank of Cooper's Creek and the south side of today's Coles Mill Road near Jobel Drive. Poet Henry Wadsworth Longfellow immortalized a romantic, but inaccurate, story about the couple's courtship in his 1873 edition of *Tales of a Wayside Inn.* (HSH.)

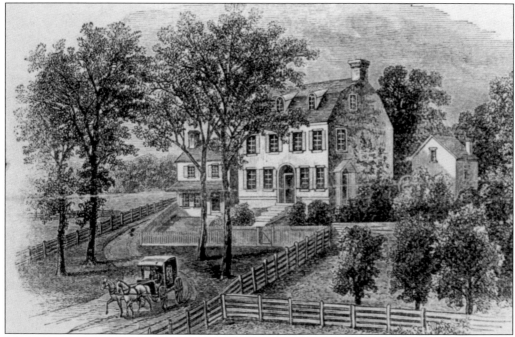

This painting reproduction depicts the second home, Haddon Hall, that John and Elizabeth Estaugh built in "New Haddonfield" in 1713. Fire destroyed this and a subsequent building. The village, which they developed by subdividing their land, grew up a short distance away and adopted the name of their plantation. Haddon Hall's approximate location is 201 Wood Lane. (HSH.)

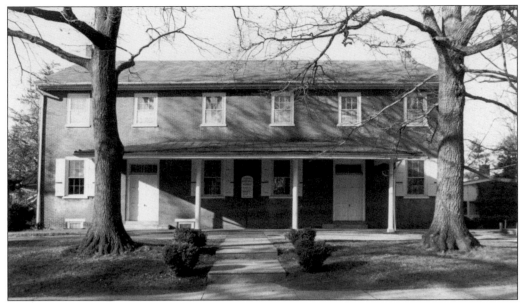

The 1721 decision of Elizabeth's father, John Haddon, to give land at the northwest corner of Kings Highway and Haddon Avenue to build a Quaker meetinghouse attracted settlers in the surrounding areas to Haddonfield for worship. The Friends' Meeting split into two groups and met separately starting in 1829. In 1851, the Orthodox group built this meetinghouse on Friends Avenue and a brick wall around its cemetery on Haddon Avenue, using brick from its original meetinghouse. (CCC&HC.)

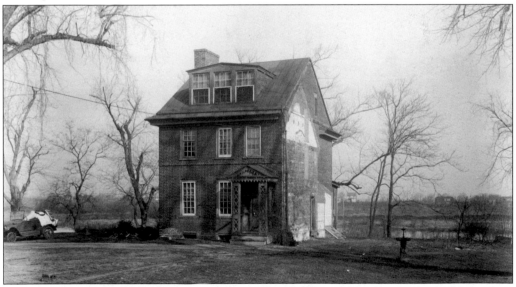

John Estaugh purchased Samuel Shriver's house on this site and gave it to Elizabeth's nephew and their "adopted son" Ebenezer Hopkins in 1737. Hopkins built the west wing (shown here) in 1740. Hopkins's daughter, Ann Burr, inherited the house, which thereafter was called Burr House. David Morgan, a photographic paper manufacturer who developed a high-quality albumen process, purchased the house and adjacent 78-acre farm in 1866. Morgan and other farmers diked and farmed the adjacent floodplain. Developer Earl Lippincott demolished the east wing in 1926. (HSH.)

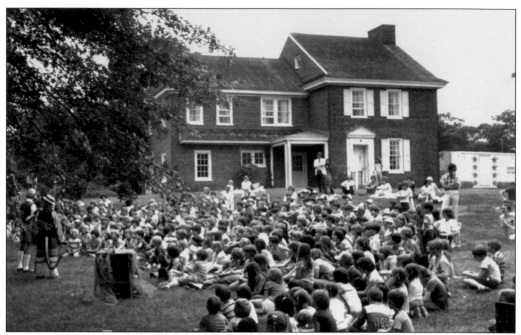

The Works Progress Administration (WPA) completed detailed architectural drawings of the Burr House as part of the Historic American Buildings Survey in 1937, prior to renovating the interior of the west wing in 1938–1939 and building a new east wing in 1939 to resemble the structure torn down in 1926. Camden County has used the Georgian brick countryseat for its park police, the Cooper River Cycle Club, an environmental study center, the county historian's office, an art gallery, and a performance venue. The county now plans to convert the Hopkins House into a dining venue surrounded by a sculpture garden. (CCC&HC.)

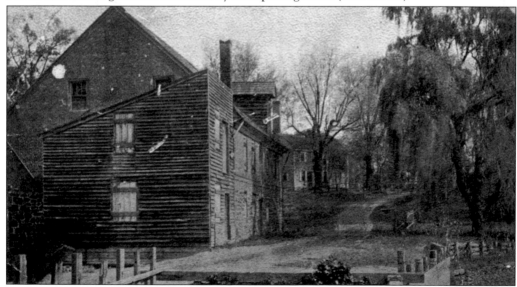

Isaac Kay built a two-story home east of his father's mill in 1747. The building, which he called Springwell, is in the center distance in this photograph, between the mill building and the willow tree. The building no longer exists, and its site on Bortons Mill Road opposite the Croft Farm in Cherry Hill is currently a parking lot. (HSH.)

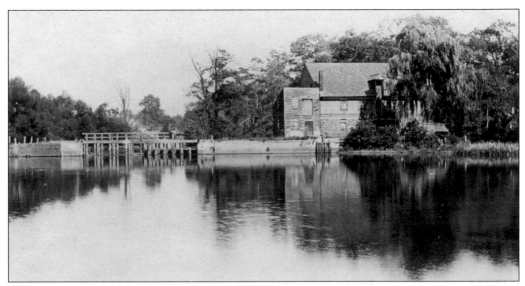

There are several old dam and mill sites in the Wallworth Park area between Cherry Hill and Haddonfield, including sites of corn mills and gristmills, a sawmill, and a fulling mill. Thomas Kendall built the first dam near here in 1697, on the south side of Cooper's Creek. John Kay built a mill damming Cooper's Creek in 1710, creating what is now called Evans Pond (pictured). The view in this photograph faces north toward the mill that Thomas Evans rebuilt in 1838 after purchasing Mathias Kay's mill in 1819. The mill passed to Thomas's son Josiah B., who, with his children, ran it under the name Josiah B. Evans & Co. In 1882, it was converted into a roller mill, processing 75 barrels of flour a day. (HSH.)

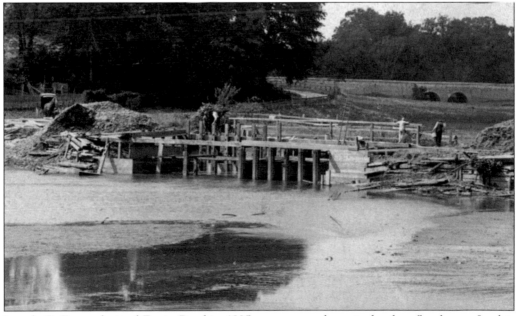

Joseph G. Evans drained Evans Pond in 1895 to renew and repair the dam floodgates. In this photograph, taken by Dr. Joseph Wills, first cousin of Mrs. J.B. Evans, William Stiles, a mill employee and son of miller Reuben C. Stiles, is on the bridge dressed in white, looking north toward the Kings Highway double-arched bridge. A single-horse carriage waits on the left. (CCHS.)

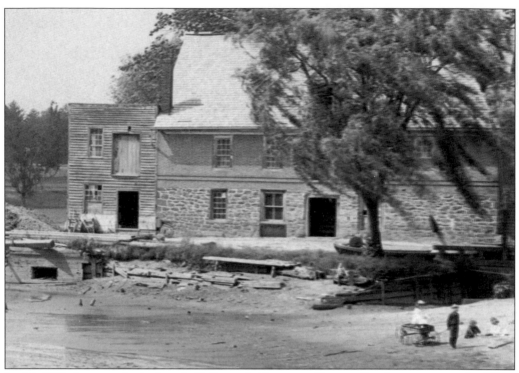

In this 1895 photograph, the Joseph G. Evans & Co. gristmill awaits floodgate repairs and refilling of Evans Pond. A waterwheel was on the right side of the mill, fed by a millrace whose opening is exposed due to the pond draining and is visible on the bottom right of this photograph, behind the children and to the right of the willow tree. The photographer's daughter, Lillian Wills, is behind the wagon. Next to her, standing, is Josiah B. Evans, son of Joseph G. Evans. Next to him, playing in the sand, are another son of Joseph G., Walter Wills Evans, and another daughter of the photographer, Helen Wills. (CCHS.)

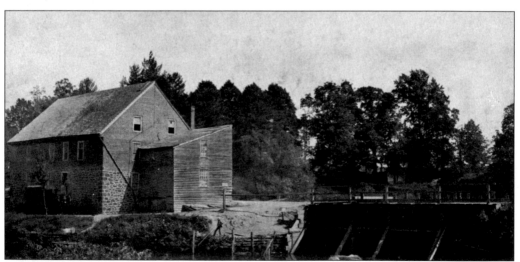

This 1902 photograph shows the site of the S.A. Willits Flour & Feed Mill, on the northeast side of the Evans Pond Dam. The Willits mill had two turbine wheels and a steam wheat heater. (CCHS.)

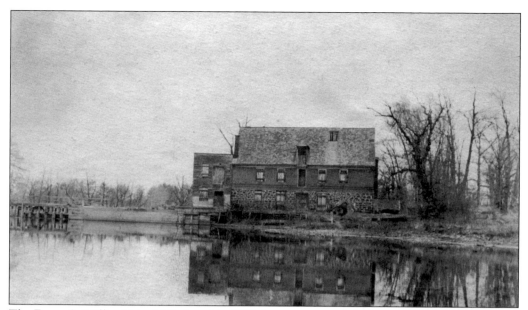

The Evans & Willits Grist Mill closed in 1897 due to a regional decline in farming as a business and because of the development of more efficient and less costly sources of milling. (HSW.)

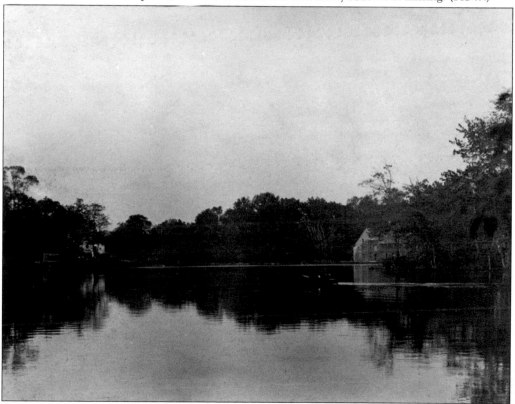

This 1891 photograph shows a man enjoying Evans Pond in a boat with double paddles headed toward the Evans Pond Dam. The mill burned down in 1913, and all its foundations are no longer visible. (HSH.)

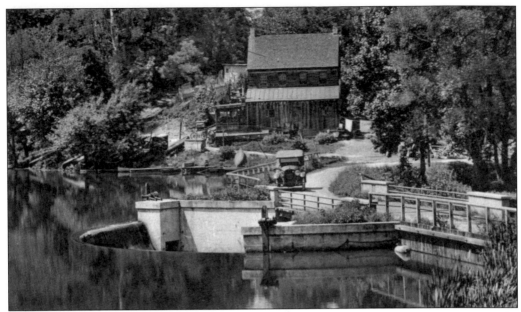

Mill employees and wagon drivers once occupied the double-framed house shown here. In the foreground is the Evans Pond Dam spillway. (HSH.)

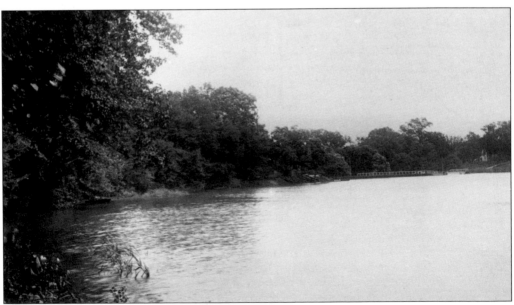

Canoes line the shore of Evans Pond west of the Evans Pond Dam. The mill employees' house is in the trees behind the canoes. (CCHS.)

Isaac Kay built the original section of the 16-room home that is now called the Croft Farm House in 1753 on high ground overlooking the millpond. It was later purchased by the Evans family. Shown here in 1888 are Mrs. Joseph G. Evans with her sons Walter Wills Evans (in the baby coach) and Josiah B. Evans (on his velocipede). S. Abbott Willits stands to the left of Mrs. Evans. A Thomas Evans descendant reported that the farmhouse was a station on the Underground Railroad and that an earlier Josiah Evans purchased the freedom of Joshua Sadler and Jefferson Fisher, two runaway slaves, who worked at his mill to repay his kindness. (CCHS.)

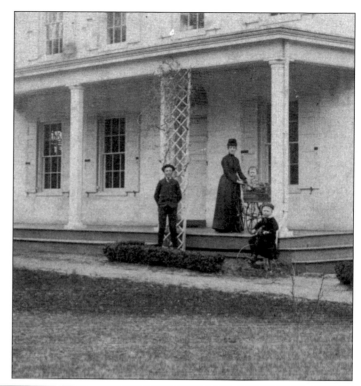

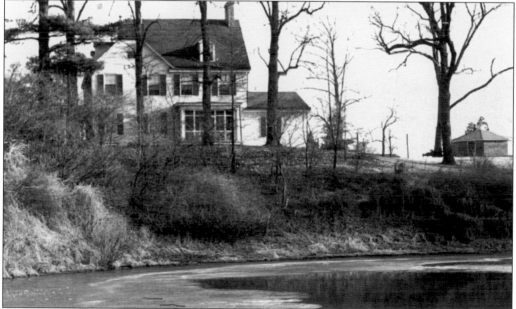

Rooms were added to the north side of the farmhouse in 1816 to change the orientation, from facing the pond to a north-looking perspective, toward Bortons Mill Road. The octagonal icehouse behind the Croft Farm House, visible at right, was designed to minimize heat gain and to store dairy and other perishables in stoneware containers. The Evans family sold the land to John Croft in the 1920s, and he farmed it until 1981. Cherry Hill Township purchased the farmhouse and 80 acres surrounding it in 1985. (CCHS.)

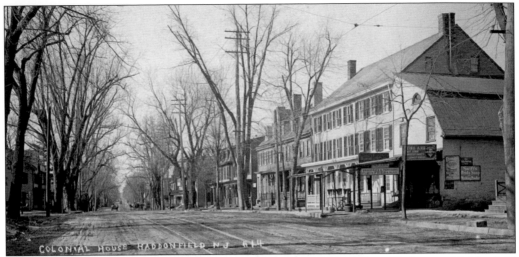

New Jersey adopted its first constitution at the Indian King Tavern on Kings Highway in Haddonfield in 1777. Quaker merchant Mathias Aspden built what later became the first state-owned historic site in 1750. A two-story structure with a mansard roof was attached to the tavern's north side in 1764. Later named the Ark (because it carried two of everything), the establishment advertised groceries and provisions, including flour, feed, hay, Swift's Pride soap and washing powder, Fels Naptha, and G.R. Butter, according to signs in this 1890 photograph. (PS.)

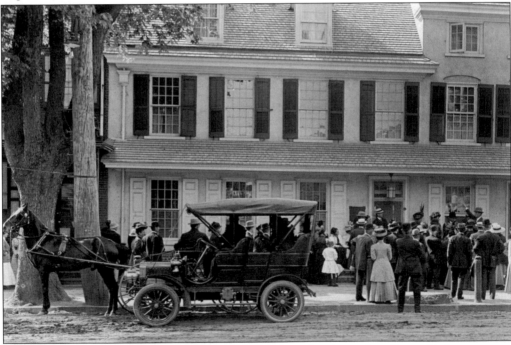

Before being convicted of treason in absentia, Mathias Aspden, a Loyalist, sold the tavern to Thomas Redman and fled to Britain in 1776. The Continental army jailed and charged Quaker pacifist Redman with sedition in 1777. When released, Redman found the state Council of Safety using his tavern to try, convict, and incarcerate deserters, Loyalists, and other enemies of the revolution. Here, the Friends Historic Society views the state's tavern renovations, including demolition of the Ark, in 1910. (CCHS.)

Haddonfield was a war zone—the British occupied the town four times after capturing Philadelphia in September 1777. Patriot generals "Mad" Anthony Wayne, the Marquis de Lafayette, and Polish count Casimir Pulaski no doubt paused at the tavern, as these Revolutionary War reenactors are doing in 2014. The British first passed through Haddonfield to attack Fort Mercer, and did so for the last time on their way to the Cooper's Creek crossing and Sandy Hook after evacuating Philadelphia in 1778. (RS.)

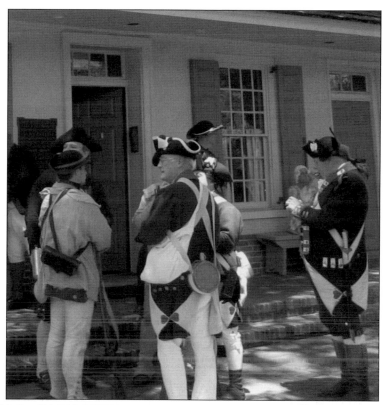

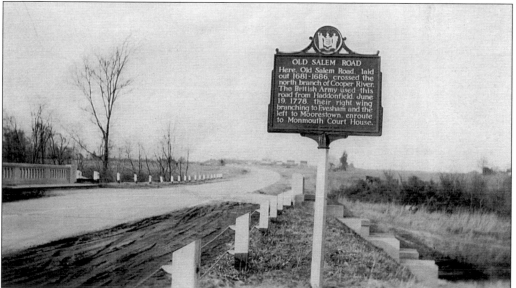

In 1681, the West Jersey General Assembly authorized a survey for a highway between Burlington and Salem. Old Salem Road allowed commerce between the two major Quaker settlements when ice blocked the Delaware River. Evacuating Philadelphia in 1778, over 15,000 British army troops marched through Haddonfield on the Kings Highway, then across Cooper's Creek near the point shown in the photograph, before going on to Freehold, where General Washington engaged them at the Battle of Monmouth. (CCHS.)

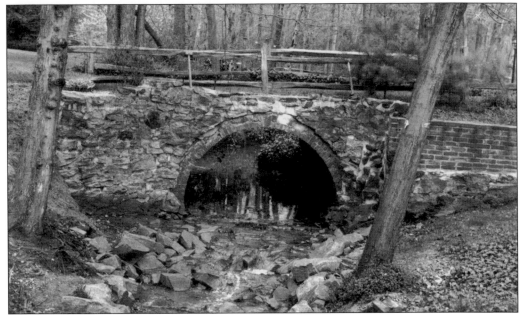

Bonnie's Bridge crosses Sawmill Creek 400 feet south of Marlton Pike (Route 70), at 350 Wayland Road in the Barclay section of Cherry Hill. A masonry-arched, handmade brick bridge 14 feet wide and 16 feet long marks the place where a road from Haddonfield to Marlton crossed the Cooper River tributary. (CCC&HC.)

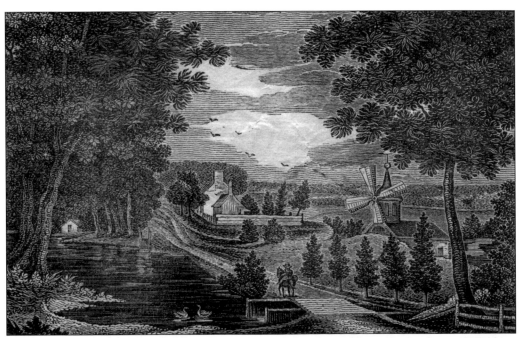

John Estaugh Hopkins built Birdwood farmhouse (center) on the northeast shore of Hopkins Pond for his son William Estaugh Hopkins in 1788. Hopkins also built a mill behind Birdwood, originally equipped with wind vanes. Lack of wind forced its conversion to waterpower. A small stream that flowed to the Cooper River was dammed, and this formed Hopkins Pond. (CCHS.)

30

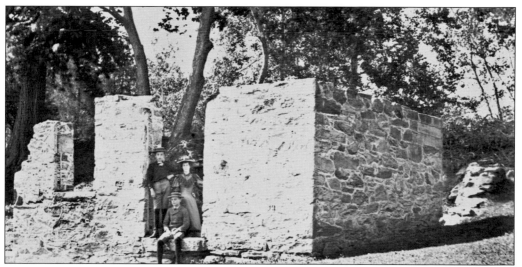

The Haddon Mill operated from 1789 until the mid-1800s. The photographs on this page show the ruins of the mill's walls and foundation, visited by two groups of Hopkins descendants—with and without their knickers. None of the walls remain on the site today. (HSH.)

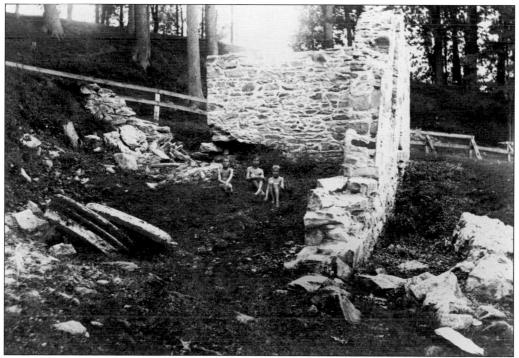

Shown here are the ruins of the Haddon Mill. Sitting in the grass that has grown in the interior of the ruins are three boys. (HSH.)

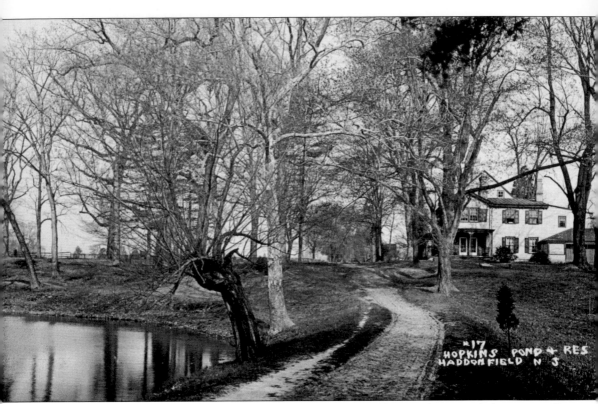

Birdwood played a central role in the discovery of the world's first dinosaur skeleton in 1858. William Hopkins invited William Parker Foulke to his house, where Foulke saw a strange bone Hopkins had found 20 years earlier. Foulke returned with scientist Joseph Leidy to excavate the pit and discovered the nearly complete skeleton of an enormous reptilian creature. Alfred E. Driscoll, New Jersey's 43rd governor (1947–1954) and president of Warner-Lambert, resided at Birdwood. (CCHS.)

This c. 1795 map shows tracts of land owned by early property holders just east of Haddonfield, near the confluence of the North and South Branches of the Cooper River. Stoys Landing is at the top center, connected by Stoys Landing Road to Haddonfield. Below and to the right of Stoys Landing are Cooperstown and Ellisburg, both located in Delaware Township (now Cherry Hill). (CCHS.)

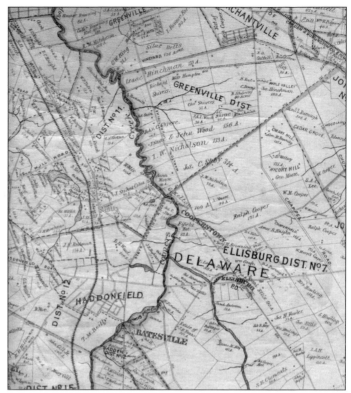

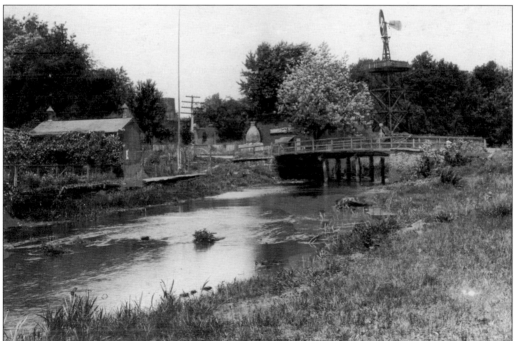

Cooper's Creek flows north under a wooden Ellis Street Bridge. The rustic Terra Cotta Works, Stewart's boat rental shed, and a windmill for pumping water line the creek's west bank in this c. 1890 photograph. (CB.)

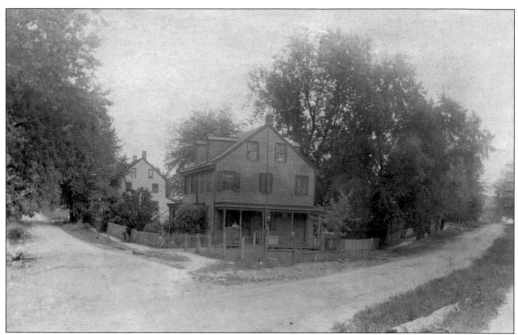

Joseph Bates built the Blazing Rag Tavern at the junction of Kresson and Berlin Roads in 1804, the year after a nearby bridge crossing the Cooper's Creek and connecting to Haddonfield was completed. The old tavern is now partially enclosed by the liquor store at this location. Early homes in Batesville were built around 1870 in typical Victorian style. (CCHS.)

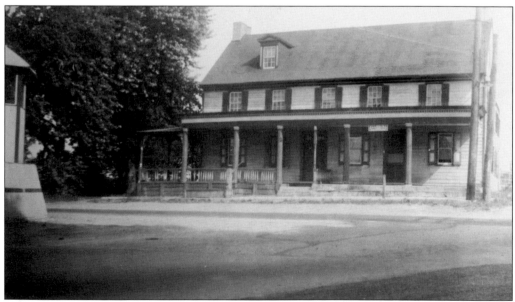

Isaac Ellis, grandson of Simeon Ellis, built a tavern at the junction of Kings Highway and the Evesham Road (Marlton Pike/Route 70) in 1795. Isaac Jr. and his son Joseph operated the tavern until 1840 as the Waterford Inn. John Ilg later purchased the tavern, which became known as the Ellisburg Inn, a popular stagecoach stop. Cherry Hill's first schoolhouse, a 16-square-foot log cabin, was built near the tavern on the Ellis property between 1750 and 1755. (HSH.)

A woman joins five men inspecting damage to the Evans Pond Dam following a damaging flood in 1895. The Evans Mill employees' house is in the background on the left. (HSH.)

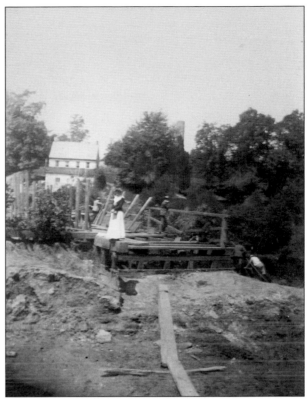

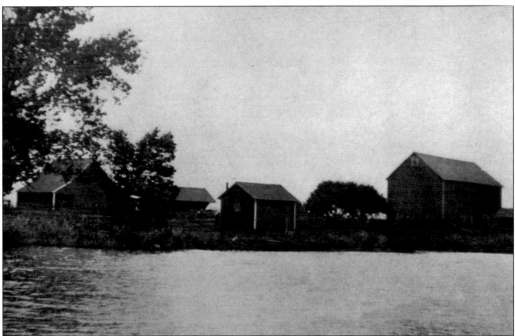

This photograph was taken from the opposite bank of Cooper's Creek in the 1920s. Barns and a farmhouse are clearly visible, showing the style of farm architecture popular at the time. (CCHS.)

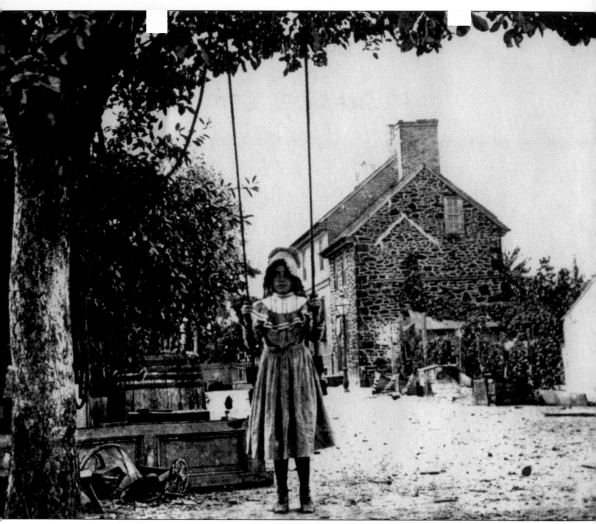

A young girl with sunbonnet sits on a tree swing in the Guenther farmyard along the Cooper River. In the background is a two-story, two-section stonemasonry house with the white outline of the roof of what was a third section of the house, since removed. A large wooden barrel with iron bands sits on the left. (CCHS.)

Three

CAMDEN INDUSTRY

Agriculture dominated the Cooper's banks until 1840, when Maurice Browning built an "Aroma Mill" in Camden to produce dyes. Industrial competition for space followed along the Cooper within the limits of Camden as development along Camden's Delaware River waterfront intensified. The Cope Paper Mill opened on the Cooper in 1845 on the future site of the M. Furbush & Son textile machinery works. Jesse and John Starr moved their ironworks from the Delaware River to the west bank of the Cooper River (where Campbell Soup's headquarters is today) in 1847.

The Cooper needed dredging between its mouth and the end of Pine Street to serve the many industries lining its banks. Over time, larger corporations acquired many of the Cooper River's early industries and shut them down when products could be produced more efficiently elsewhere. As technology changed, other manufactures either lost markets for their products or lost competitive advantage to others. The industrial enterprises and chemical works gradually disappeared from the Cooper's banks, with all waterborne movements ending in 1982.

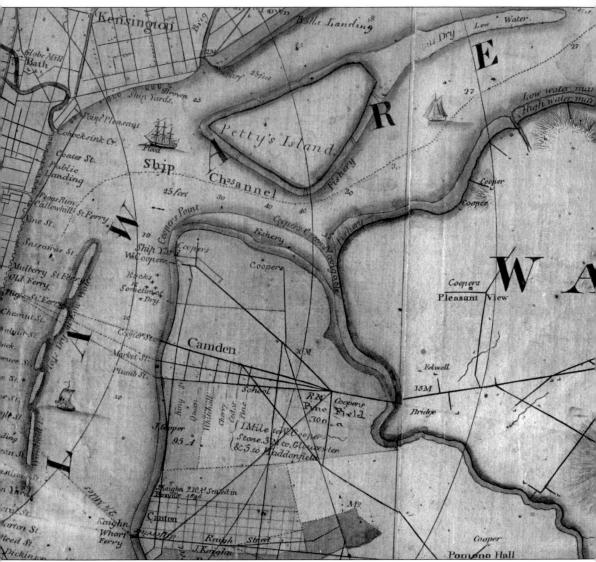

Ferries and fisheries were Camden's first industries, as shown on this c. 1810 map. Fishermen caught shad by the ton along the shore near the confluence of the Cooper and Delaware Rivers. John McPhee's *The Founding Fish* describes the shad's role in nourishing George Washington's army at Valley Forge and traces the shad's demise. The shad harvest peaked in the early 1900s, then began to collapse from overfishing and river pollution. (CCHS.)

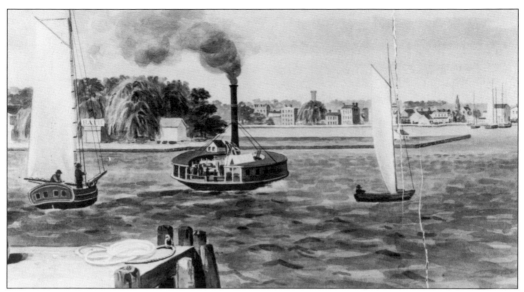

In this c. 1810 illustration, a ferry steams away from Camden between two sailboats on its way to Philadelphia. (CCHS.)

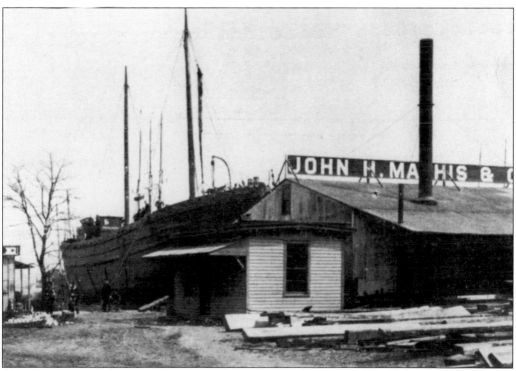

The John H. Mathis shipyard is operated north of the Delaware River Bridge, near Coopers Point, shown in this 1901 photograph. British lieutenant colonel Abercrombie used the Mathis office building as his headquarters in 1777–1778. Mathis built tugs, trawlers, barges, cargo vessels, minesweepers, net tenders, tankers, car floats, lightships, landing craft, and a hospital ship. Weeks Marine now occupies the site. (CCHS.)

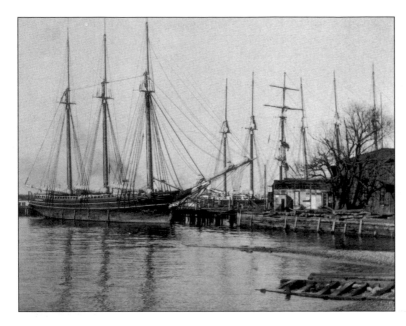

In this c. 1890 photograph, three tall ships are docked along the Delaware River between the Mathis shipyard and Cooper's Creek. The remains of a wooden shipway for repairs and launchings is visible in the foreground, on the lower right. (PS.)

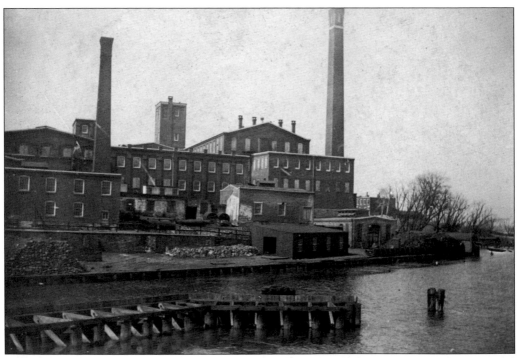

The Highland Worsted Mills started as the Camden Woolen Mill during the Civil War, but it did not begin operation until just three months before Confederate general Robert E. Lee surrendered in April 1865. The owners built the mill to get a share of the federal government's lucrative wool uniform contracts. The mill was raided during Prohibition, when bootleggers had converted it into a liquor distillery. The mill was demolished in the 1960s, and the site has been redeveloped into townhouses. (PS.)

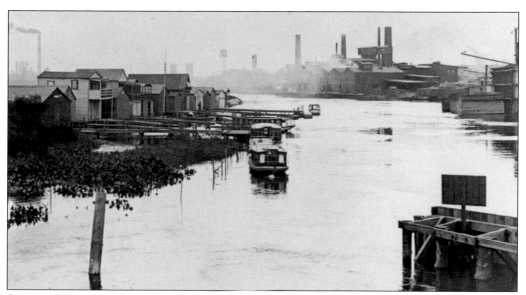

Summer houses with boat docks line the east bank of Cooper's Creek, in this view facing south from the State Street Bridge. Joseph Wharton's Camden Nickel Works and other Camden industries are along the Cooper's west bank, in the background. (CCHS.)

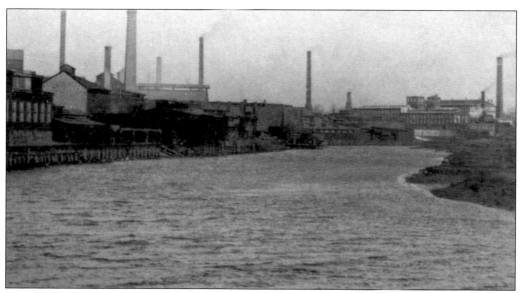

Seen here are, from left to right, the American Nickel Works, the Wharton Glass Works, and the Highland Woolen Mill. Francis Buck and William Coffin started making nickel and cobalt in Camden in 1853, after Coffin and Philadelphia Mint official James C. Booth found an efficient method to produce the first nickel coins. Philadelphia Quaker and industrialist Joseph Wharton recognized the economic return of owning the only commercial nickel refinery in North America and purchased the works in 1864. His company produced nearly 20 percent of world nickel output in 1877. In 1902, Wharton sold to the American Nickel Works Company, which ended nickel production in Camden in 1906. (CCHS.)

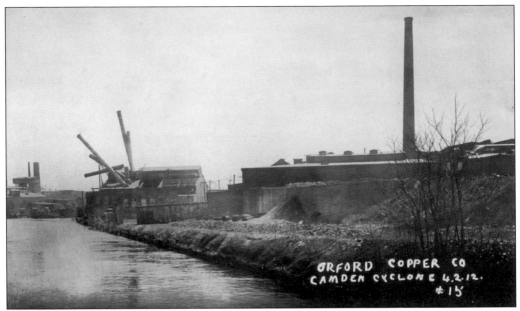

A 1912 tornado knocked five smokestacks over "like so many tenpins," as seen in this photograph at the Oxford Copper works, formerly Wharton's nickel refinery, in Camden at Elm and Tenth Streets. William W. Fleming, who built the first US nickel refinery in 1848 upstream from Wharton's site, did not enjoy Wharton's success. Other investment losses forced Fleming to disappear and to be declared legally dead. He later reunited with his wife in Belgium, living comfortably on funds left by her father, Samuel Richards, a New Jersey iron furnace magnate. (PS.)

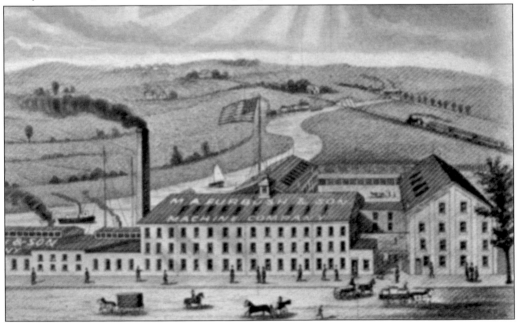

This drawing portrays Furbush Machine Works, built on the site of the 1845 Cope Paper Mill. Furbush converted the site to a machine shop in 1863, manufacturing wool textile equipment. The plant continued to operate until 1924. The Camden & Amboy Railroad and Federal Street bridges cross Cooper's Creek in the background. (CCHS.)

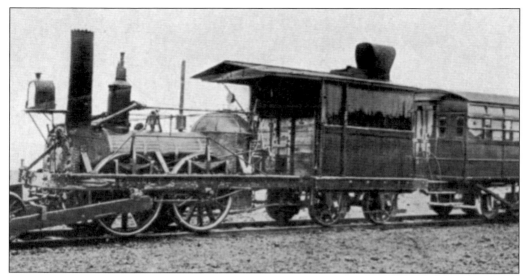

The Camden & Amboy Railroad (C&A), the first railroad in New Jersey, gave the British-built John Bull locomotive (pictured) the number *1* and called it *Stevens*. The C&A used *Stevens* heavily from 1833 until 1866. The railroad terminated on the Camden waterfront, and passengers were ferried across the Delaware River to Philadelphia. The C&A helped to spur an increase in population and commerce in Camden. (CCHS.)

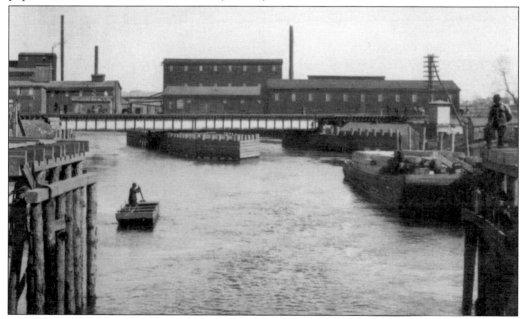

The C&A constructed its first swing-span railroad bridge across Cooper's Creek in 1834 with great difficulty, given the soft soil conditions of the adjacent meadows at the location shown here. In this photograph, with a view facing north from the Federal Street Bridge under construction, a man in a scow is visible on the left. The Pennsylvania Railroad built a railroad bridge over Cooper's Creek in 1891 at this location, with a double-track, open-deck, plate-girder, center-pivot swing bridge and a new east approach span in the 1940s, replacing timber trestles with a steel bridge. The railroad bridge could be opened for Cooper River traffic until the early 1980s, when it was pinned closed. (CCHS.)

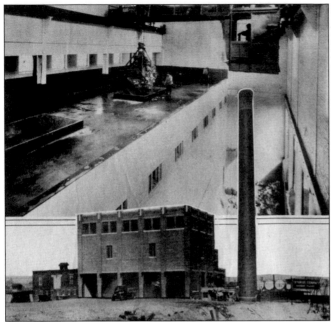

These 1920s-era photographs show Camden's trash incinerator inside and out. The remains of the incinerator remain on the Cooper River's west bank, between the Federal Street Bridge and the railroad bridge. (CB.)

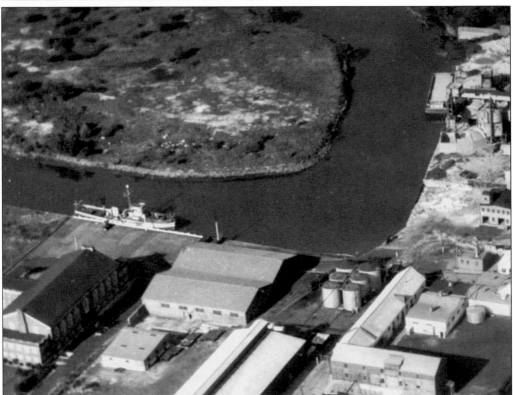

John and Jesse Starr purchased land from the Richard M. Cooper estate in 1847 to construct the Camden Iron Works at the location south of the Admiral Wilson Boulevard (Route 30) bridge where the Cooper River makes a sharp turn. The peaked roof building shown at the bottom in the middle of the photograph are on the site today. (CCHS.)

The Starrs operated the Camden Iron Works until 1883, when the R.D. Wood Company gained control. R.D. Wood manufactured gas distribution equipment and pipe. The two-masted tall sailing vessel and other river barges transported R.D. Wood's products to market. R.D. Wood manufactured gas distribution equipment and the pipe stowed on the dock next to the two-masted tall sailing vessel and other river barges it used to transport its products to market. The Wood facility went bankrupt in 1917. The City of Camden purchased the site by 1920 for a civic center it never built. The city converted one of the large ironworks casting sheds into a convention hall that was used until it burned down in a 1953 fire. (CCHS.)

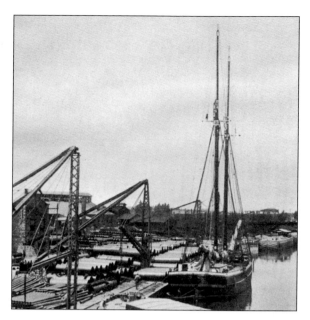

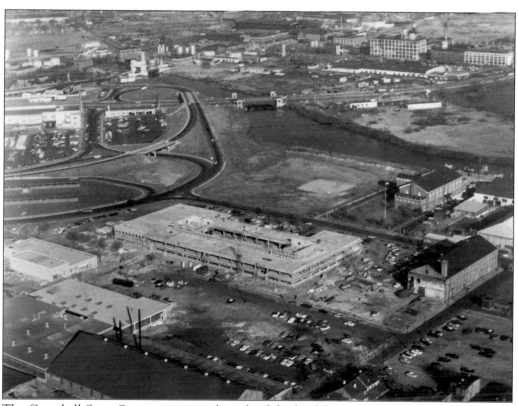

The Campbell Soup Company acquired much of the land formerly occupied by the Starr and R.D. Wood ironworks to build test kitchens and research laboratories in the 1950s, as shown in this photograph. Campbell subsequently built the company's world headquarters between the Cooper River and research labs in the open space shown here. (CCHS.)

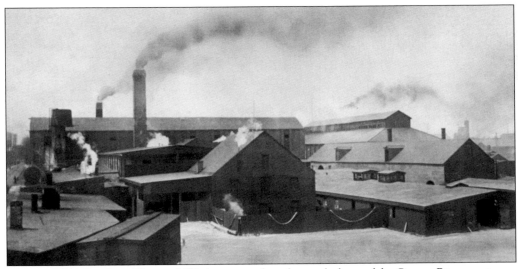

The Mechling Brothers Chemical Works operated on the south shore of the Cooper River, upstream (west) of the former Camden Iron Works site. This site had many industrial owners, beginning with the Sassackon Chemical Works in the late 1840s, succeeded by Potts & Klett, which produced chemicals and fertilizers in the 1850s. The New Jersey Chemical Company acquired the plant in 1872, then sold it to Mechling Brothers, a Philadelphia drug and spice company. (CCHS.)

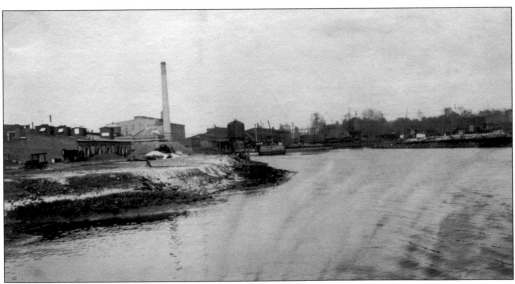

This south-facing view includes the smokestack of the West Jersey Manufacturing Company. A fertilizer factory building is on the left, and a barge is tied up to the Camden Lime Company's dock, east of the Mechling Brothers. A landfill with white material on the north shore peninsula juts south of Admiral Wilson Boulevard. At left, a horse is harnessed to a two-wheeled wagon, and another wagon works the landfill. (CCHS.)

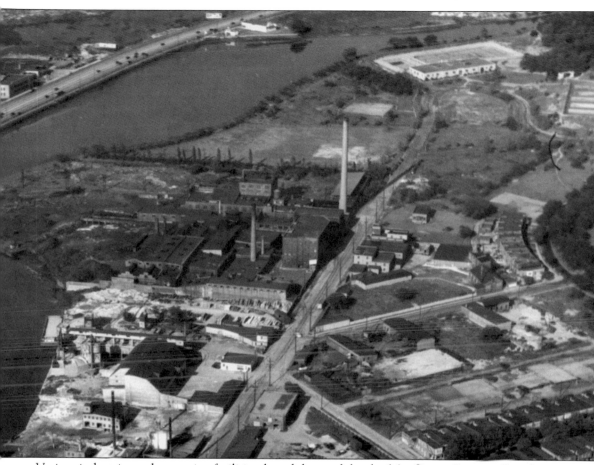

Various industries and recreation facilities shared the south bank of the Cooper River in Camden along Pine Street. Pine Street runs from the white rectangular New Camden Park municipal pool and bathing complex in the upper right corner of this aerial photograph west on a diagonal (down and to the left to the middle of the image). The dye-producing Taylor-White Extracting Company is west of the bathing complex to the left of the tallest smokestack. The Wilckes Lampblack Factory, to the right of the smaller smokestack and west of Taylor-White's facility, produced carbon for printer's ink and rubber products. Monsanto acquired the factory around 1930. Fire destroyed the plant in 1976. West Jersey Manufacturing's fertilizer factory was to the west (left of Wilkes Lampblack) and operated between 1905 and 1913. The Browning Brothers/Camden Lime Company facility is in the foreground (bottom left) with a river barge tied to its wharf near a pile of white-colored material. Maurice Browning built one of Camden's earliest factories, the so-called Aroma Mills, on this site in 1840. The factory extracted dyes from dyewoods to produce brown and white sugar of lead and pyroligneous acid (also called wood vinegar). The Aroma Mills plant ground and fermented dyewoods and transferred them to Potts & Klett (later Mechling Brothers) downriver for final processing. Campbell Soup Company acquired all of the former industrial sites shown here by 1988. (CCHS.)

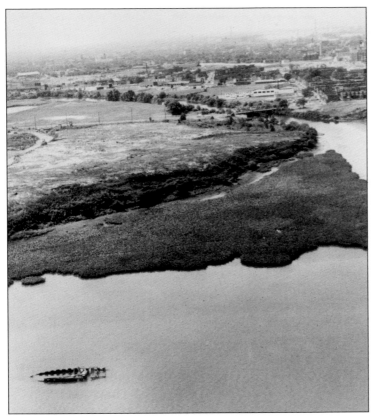

The north bank of the mouth of the Cooper River was a large meadow before it was filled with dredge spoils and residue from the Moro Phillips chemical works in the early 20th century. The North Camden Airport opened on the same site in 1919. Hundreds of people attending an air show at the airport are shown in the photograph below. Nearby factory smokestacks limited visibility and the airport's usefulness. It closed when Central Airport opened in Pennsauken in1929. The site later became the Harrison Avenue Landfill for city of Camden trash. (Both, CCHS..)

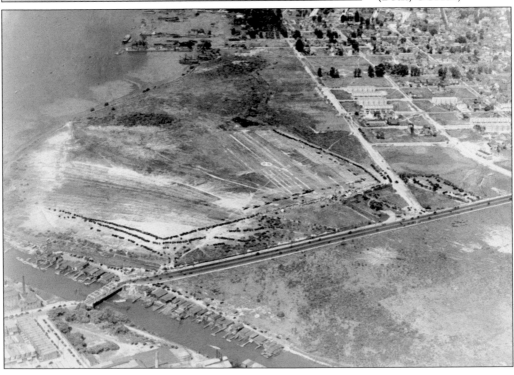

Four

FERRIES AND THE DELAWARE RIVER BRIDGE

Delaware River ferries linked South Jersey to Philadelphia through Camden for 250 years. The first ferries in the late 17th century carried Quakers across the Delaware River to alternating monthly meetings at William Cooper's house at Pyne Poynt and Thomas Fairman's house at Shackamaxon (directly across from Coopers Point, where Penn's Treaty Park is located today). For the first 150 years, Camden served as a secondary economic and transportation hub for the Philadelphia area. That status began to change in the early 19th century, when one of the United States' first railroads, the Camden & Amboy Railroad, was chartered in 1830 (see page 43). The Cooper Street ferry was the first to operate, in 1688. William Cooper bought and transferred ownership to his son Daniel in 1695. William gave son Joseph the Coopers Point ferry in 1708. Coopers Point remained in the family until 1872, when the Camden & Atlantic Railroad bought it. The Pennsylvania Railroad Company purchased it in 1883. During the 1870s and before consolidation, a total of six ferryboat companies operated between Camden and Philadelphia. The construction of the Delaware River Bridge between Camden and Philadelphia and the rise of automobile use doomed the ferries and the trains that served them. This chapter travels back to the heyday of the ferries before returning to the brink of their extinction.

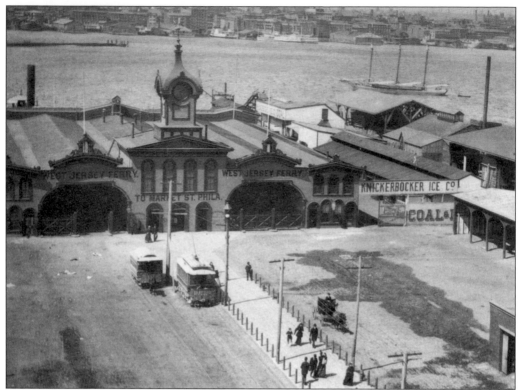

The West Jersey Ferry terminal in Camden, originally designed by Stephen Decatur Button for the Philadelphia Centennial Exhibition, is seen here around 1895. Abraham Browning Sr., a Stockton Township farmer whose father-in-law had a boatyard at the foot of Camden's Market Street, began the West Jersey Ferry in 1800. The Pennsylvania Railroad Company bought the ferry in 1883. (CCHS.)

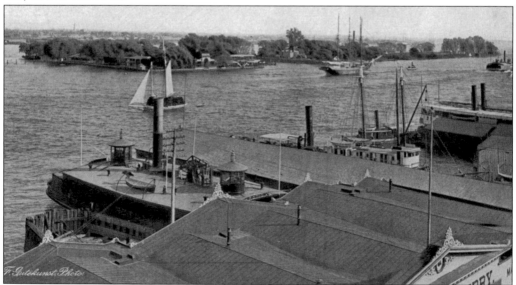

The Pennsylvania Railroad's Market Street Ferry connected Camden's Federal Street terminal to the Market Street terminal in Philadelphia. (CCHS.)

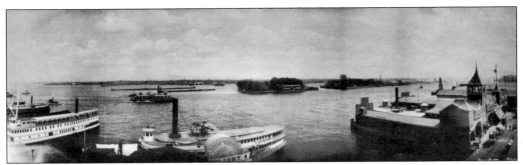

The Camden and Philadelphia Steamboat Company began ferry operations in 1836 from a terminals at Bridge Avenue in Camden and at Chestnut Street in Philadelphia. The company ended long detours around Windmill Island by cutting a canal across the island in 1838. This photograph shows the Windmill Island cut, to the right and above the *Twilight* side-wheeler riverboat in the foreground. (CCHS.)

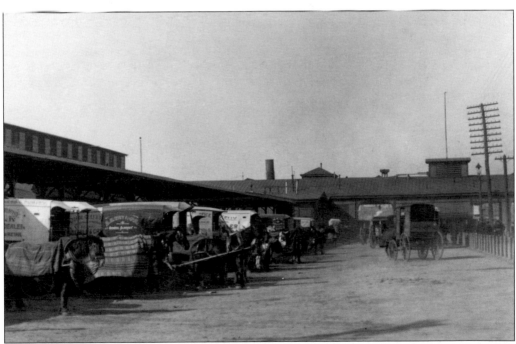

A typical day at the Camden Federal Street Ferry started with milk wagons lined up to be pulled onto the ferry, as shown here. An 1887 article observed, "The early morning is ushered in with the rattling of milk cans being conveyed from the railroads to the wagons in waiting, where their contents will soon be distributed to thousands of people. . . . The travelers are mostly of the laboring classes . . . decked out in blue overalls and jumpers, ready for the toil of the day." (HSH.)

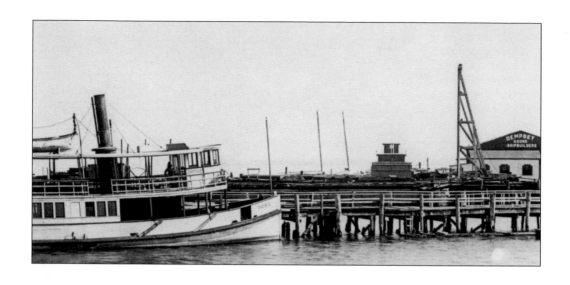

In the early 1890s, the North Cramer Hill Ferry Company organized to provide commuter service for Camden residents to get to industries in the Kensington district of Philadelphia and for Philadelphians to access New Jersey parks. One of the North Cramer Hill Ferry Company's ferries, the *Eastside*, is shown above. On the right is the Dempsey and Sons Shipbuilders building. The company's ferry, *Pyne Point*, is shown in the below photograph. These ferries and the pedestrian-only little steamer *Riverside* carried passengers for 25 years. (Both, PS.)

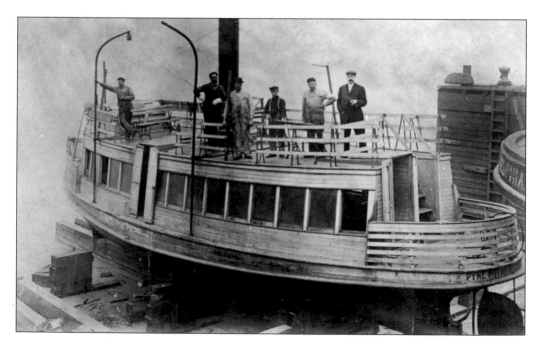

In 1818, Edward Sharp proposed the earliest plan to bridge the Delaware River between Camden and Philadelphia. As shown here, Sharp proposed to construct a wooden bridge from Camden to Windmill Island. Travelers would complete passage to Philadelphia on a short ferry trip from the southern end of the island. Sharp was unable to raise sufficient capital to begin construction. His proposed Bridge Avenue is now Cooper Street in Camden. (CCHS.)

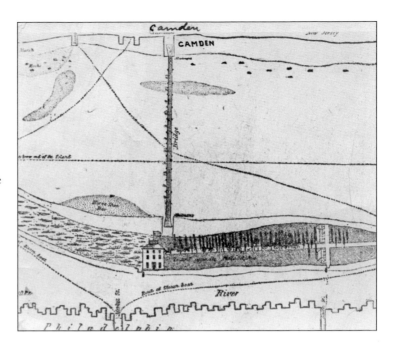

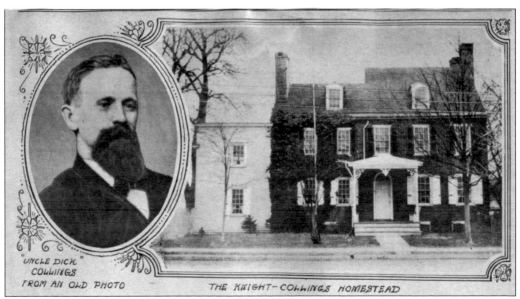

Richard Collings is known as the "Father of the Delaware Bridge." Collings was a mayor of Collingswood, New Jersey, in 1908 and a member of one of its founding families. Along with Edward C. Knight, he pioneered the concept of building public parks to attract buyers of their residential development projects in Camden County. Collings relentlessly pushed for laws to permit preliminary planning for the bridge. He assembled a group of Burlington County farmers to complain about ferry service to their county freeholders and to persuade them to reverse their earlier opposition to the bridge. Collings died in 1920, before Pennsylvania and New Jersey finally committed to building the bridge. (CB.)

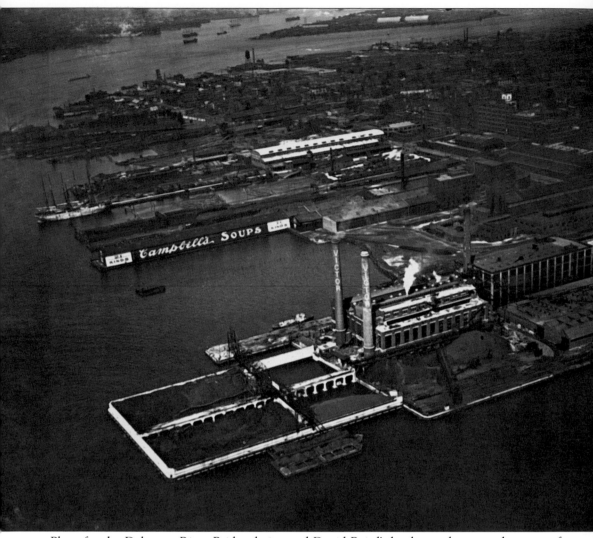

Plans for the Delaware River Bridge designated David Baird's lumber and spar yard as part of the right-of-way needed on the Camden side. Seen here in 1925 is Baird's yard on the Delaware River waterfront, north of the Campbell Soup and Victor Talking Machine properties. Baird, an Irish immigrant, started his Camden business in 1872 and came to dominate Camden County politics. Baird did not oppose the plan to take his lumber and spar yard for the bridge right-of-way. (LCP.)

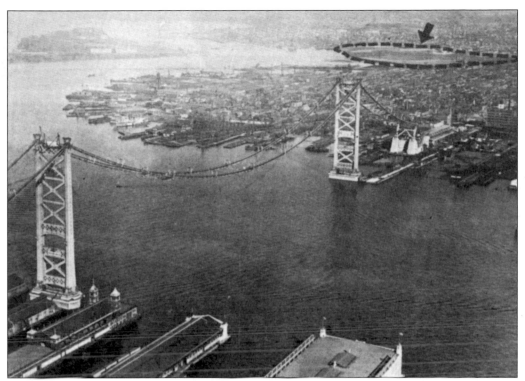

At the time it was constructed, the Delaware River Bridge was the longest suspension bridge in the world. Seen in this aerial view looking east from Philadelphia, the bridge towers are 382 feet tall. Strung over them are two 30-inch-diameter cable bundles, each holding 18,666 wire strands. The mouth of the Cooper River and the proposed North Camden airport site are shown in the upper right. Petty's Island is at upper left. (CCHS.)

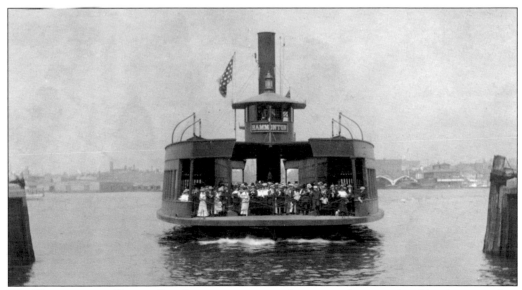

The *Hammonton* pulls into Camden as men in straw boaters and women in white dresses gather at the safety gates. (CCHS.)

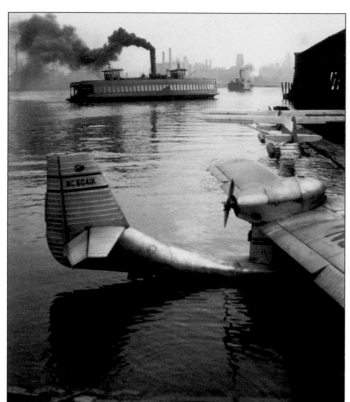

The *Haddonfield* blows steam through its boilers and spews smoke from its stack as the captain applies power on its way to Camden. A seaplane is moored to a Philadelphia dock in the foreground. (CCHS.)

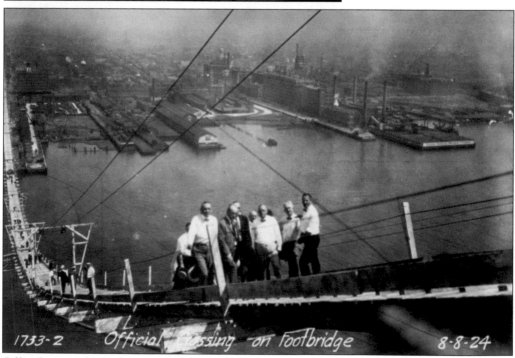

Officials cross the Delaware River toward Philadelphia on a footbridge between the towers on August 8, 1924. The Camden waterfront is in the background. (CCHS.)

56

Bridge officials sponsored two opening ceremonies for the Delaware River Bridge. The first, shown here, occurred on July 1, 1926, when the bridge was opened for over 100,000 pedestrians. A second ceremony, held on July 5, 1926, was attended by Pres. Calvin Coolidge. (CCHS.)

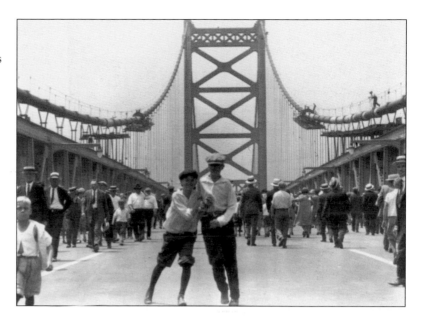

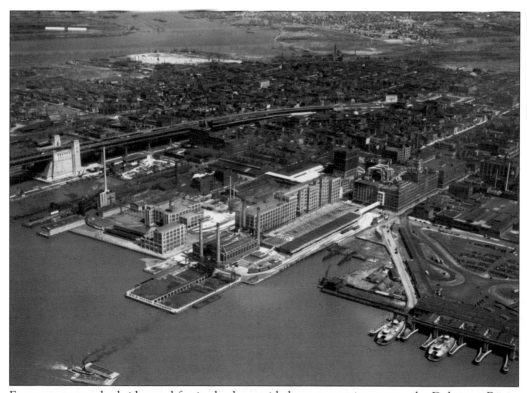

For some years, the bridge and ferries both provided transportation across the Delaware River. The bridge handled automobiles and streetcars, and the ferries mostly carried passengers arriving and departing by train. Gradually, bridge use replaced the ferries. Ferry service between Camden's Vine Street and Vine and Shackamaxon Streets in Philadelphia ceased operation in October 1926, three months after the Delaware River Bridge opened. (LCP.)

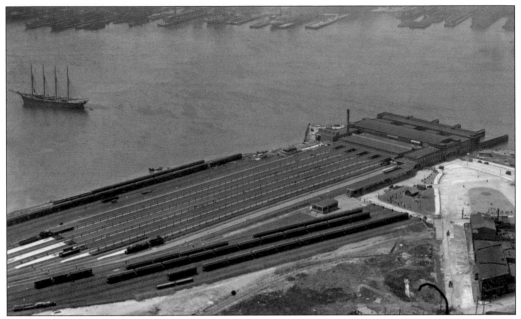

The South Camden Ferry Company, organized by Charles and Joseph M. Kaighn, built a terminal at the foot of Kaighn Avenue in 1853. After financial difficulties, this ferry passed through several hands until it was acquired by the Philadelphia & Reading Railway Company in 1888. The railroad completed a new ferry at Kaighn Avenue (pictured) while the bridge was under construction. (SCRCTUL.)

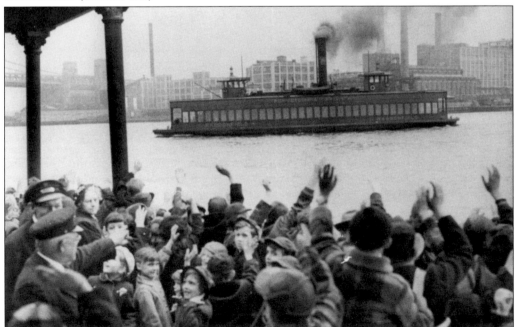

All ferry service from Camden ended in March 1952. Here, passengers bid the ferry *Haddonfield* good-bye on its last crossing. The Camden waterfront is in the background. The Delaware River Bridge, renamed the Ben Franklin Bridge on January 17, 1956 (the 250th anniversary of Franklin's birth), is in the background at left. (CCCH&C.)

Five

RECREATION ALONG THE COOPER RIVER

Before the 20th century, most American men and women worked long hours, six days a week, with little time or surplus resources to spend on recreation. The industrial revolution and new transportation modes provided opportunities for city dwellers to spend their leisure time along the Cooper River.

This chapter traces the evolution of those activities, from people-watching on city park benches to community bathing in public pools. It provides a window on how demands for the amount and type of recreation changed. Later chapters illustrate how park planners reflected those changed demands in their designs and what planners hoped to accomplish with their new park designs.

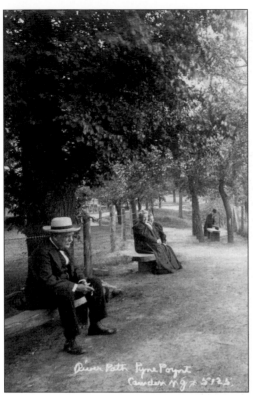

Camden residents relax in Pyne Poynt Park. The park experienced a steady demise starting in the late 1960s, but it was redeveloped into an active recreation site with sports fields in 2013. (PS.)

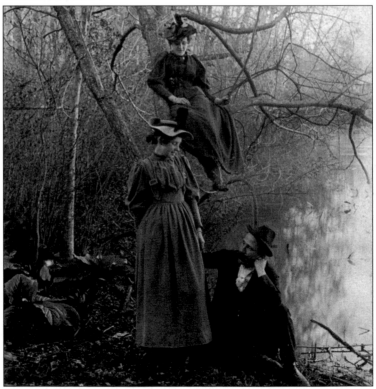

These people enjoy the serenity of the woods around Hopkins Pond in Haddonfield. (HSH.)

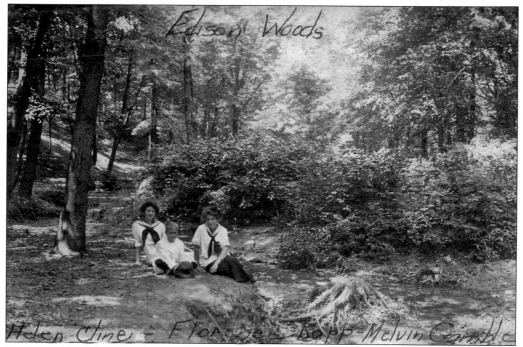

In this c. 1910 photograph, Helen Cline (left), Florence Rapp (right), and Melvin Gamble sit on the banks of a Cooper River tributary in Haddon Township. Residents of the Westmont neighborhood of Haddon Township called this park area Edison Woods. (CCLS.)

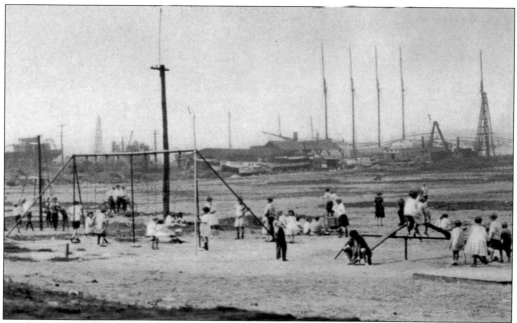

Here, boys and girls enjoy, from left to right, a maypole, swing set, and seesaw in a basic Pyne Point playground. The Mathis Shipyard is in the background. Half of a large ship is visible on the left, and four masts of a schooner are on the right. (HSW.)

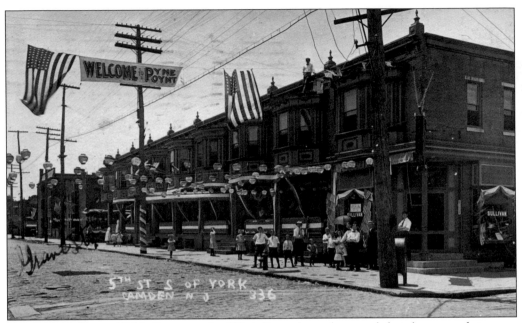

Patriotic residents of Fifth Street south of York Street have decorated their homes and strung a "Welcome to Pyne Poynt" banner over their street. The people are dressed up, with all the men and boys wearing ties, perhaps prepared to welcome a dignitary. Block after block of Camden's residential neighborhoods were built with these types of row houses, with a store or saloon at the end of the street. (PS.)

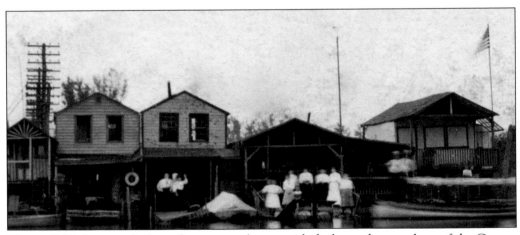

This c. 1900 photograph shows five summer homes with docks on the east shore of the Cooper River in Camden, near the State Street Bridge. The boat on the right tied to the dock of the house flying the American flag has a canopy and may have been used to give river tours. (CCHS.)

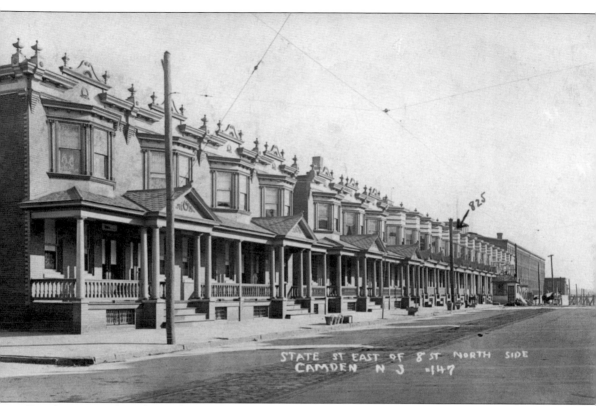

STATE ST EAST OF 8 ST NORTH SIDE
CAMDEN N J •147

Row houses are for sale on the north side of Camden's State Street, east of Eighth Street. This location is adjacent to the Highland Worsted Mill on the south side of the State Street Bridge (far right), which crosses the Cooper River. Residents sought recreation away from these homes, especially on hot summer days. An early version of an on-site real estate sales office, advertising "Houses for Sale," is on the far end of the row. (PS.)

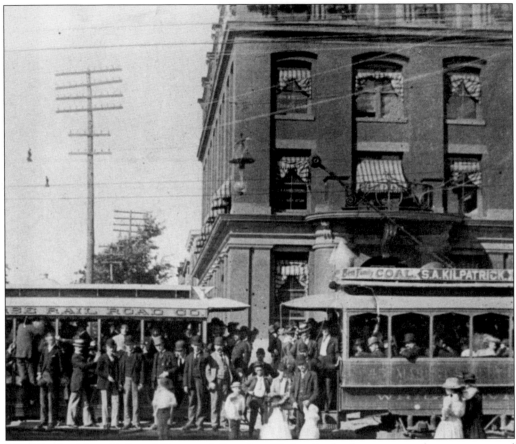

The Camden Horse Railroad Company's first electrified trolley loads passengers downtown around 1889. Camden Horse was built in 1871 to connect city points with the ferries to Philadelphia. A syndicate purchased the Camden Horse in 1889, converted it to electricity, and extended the line out Federal Street to Wrightsville. Developers built row houses in areas near the trolleys. (CCC&HC.)

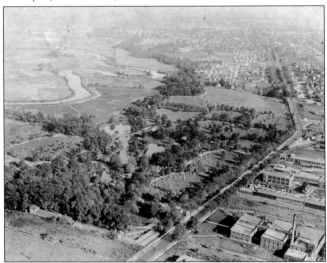

Camden's residents often visited Harleigh Cemetery, a Victorian-era garden cemetery and one of the oldest cemeteries in New Jersey. Harleigh was designed as a place of public entertainment on Camden's western border. (CCHS.)

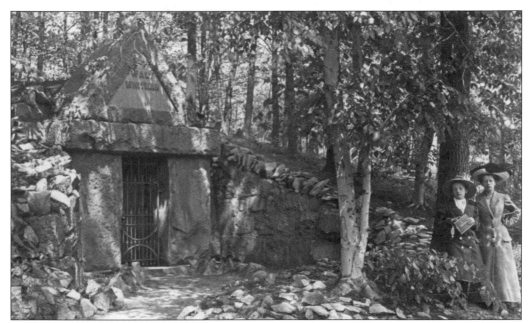

Walt Whitman, the great American poet, designed his tomb to resemble an etching by poet William Blake. Here, women in Victorian dress visit Whitman's tomb around 1900. Whitman moved to Camden in 1873, where he completed the sixth and final edition of his book of poems, *Leaves of Grass*, in 1881. Ralph Waldo Emerson found Whitman's book to be "the most extraordinary piece of wit and wisdom America has yet contributed." (PS.)

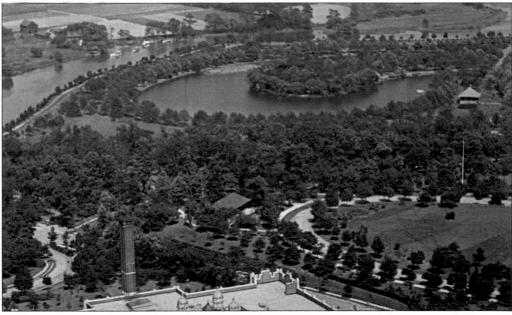

The City of Camden bought 80 acres east of Baird Boulevard in 1904 for Forest Hill Park. City engineer Levi Farnham designed the park with a lake and its own island (upper right). Farnham's plan included stone bridges to the island and the pavilion near the lake's edge (center right). The Hatch Farm and barns are visible at the upper left. Camden High School is on the lower left. The city renamed the park Farnham Park in 1927 to honor its former engineer. (LCP.)

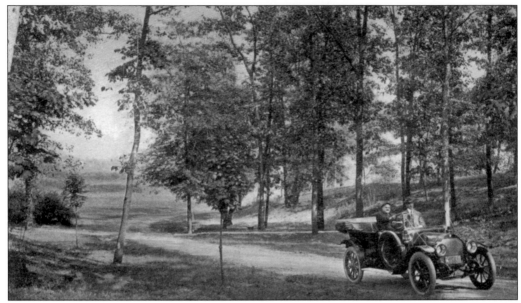

Two unidentified men drive through Forrest Hill Park in this undated postcard view. Seen in the background are walking paths, benches, and both young and mature trees. (PS.)

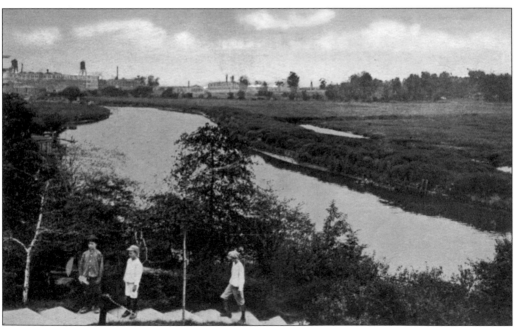

This postcard view of the Cooper River and Camden shows three boys climbing steps to the top of Red Hill in Forest Hill (Farnham) Park near Baird Boulevard Bridge. From left to right in the background are the brick buildings of the Camden Iron Works, the white buildings of the Cooper Hospital, the city trash incinerator chimney, low buildings belonging to N.Z. Graves, and the General Chemical Company. The New Jersey Highway Department constructed Admiral Wilson Boulevard through the wetlands and tidal marshes on the right. (PS.)

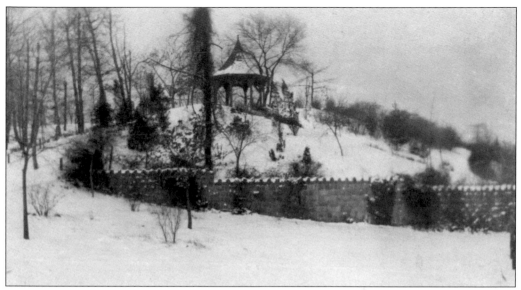

Farnham Park's Red Hill, also known as Ward's Hill, was formed during the Ice Age, when the sun's rays melted the Cooper River's east bank faster than the west bank. Camden's park commission constructed the gazebo shown at the top of Red Hill. Camden County constructed a half-sized replica of this gazebo at Challenge Grove Park in Cherry Hill. The Camden City Park Commission also erected a white marble statue of Gen. George Washington praying at Valley Forge on top of Red Hill. Officials moved the statue to the Justice Center in downtown Camden in 1985 to protect it from vandalism. (PS.)

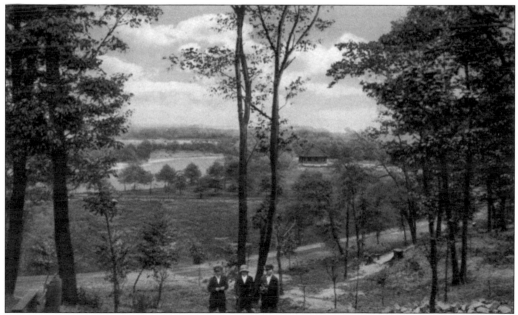

This postcard view of Forest Hill Park from Red Hill shows the lake and an octagonal brick pavilion on the lake's west shore in the background. The Cooper River flows behind the embankment on the far lakeshore to the left. In the early 1970s, Hurricane Agnes caused the Cooper River to breach the lake's retaining banks, allowing the river to repeatedly flood and, over the years, slowly destroy the lake portion of the park and undermine the now iconic brick pavilion. (PS.)

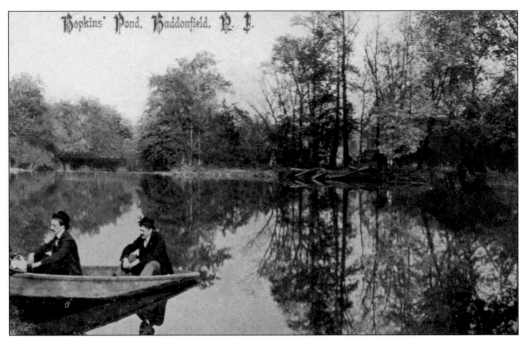

In this west-facing view, two unidentified men with hats, coats, and ties sit in a rowboat against the shore of Hopkins Pond in Haddonfield. A bridge is visible in the distance above and between the men. (HSH.)

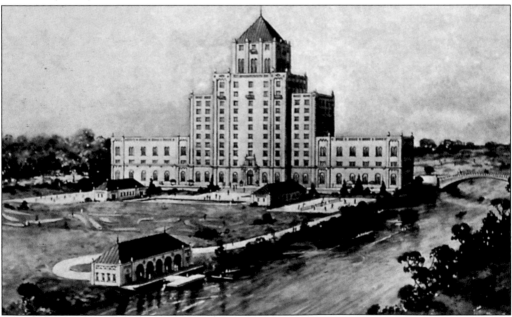

Eldridge Johnson, founder and chief executive officer of the Victor Talking Machine Company, led a civic effort among Camden's business elites to fund a City Athletic Center designed by Delaware River Bridge architect Paul Cret and depicted in this 1928 rendering. Part of the Athletic Center was built south of Admiral Wilson Boulevard and west of the Baird Boulevard Bridge. The 1929 stock market crash curtailed completion of the center. By 1947, the YMCA was using the building. (HSW.)

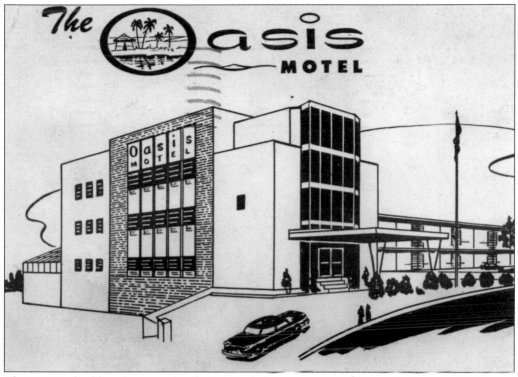

The YMCA building became the Oasis Motel, featuring go-go dancers in the early 1970s and attracting a variety of vices until 2000. Gov. Christie Whitman demolished the seedy establishments south of Admiral Wilson Boulevard to impress national Republican leaders at their 2000 Philadelphia convention. As Camden history chronicler Phil Cohen observed, it was "a sad end for a building that had been erected with such high hopes." (PS.)

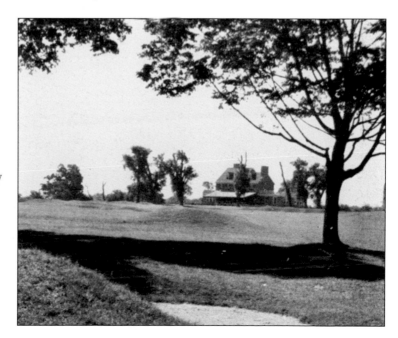

In the early 1900s, a golf course replaced a horse-racing track on the north bank of the Cooper River near the old Browning Road Bridge. The course was later renamed the Cooper Valley Country Club, which replaced the old clubhouse by converting the farmhouse shown here on the right behind a sand trap in the foreground. The club's course was located east of the Airport Circle. (CCHS.)

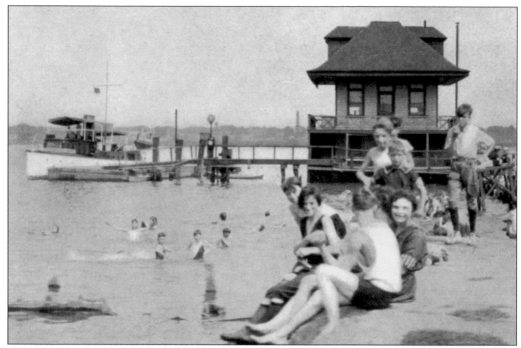

This c. 1910 photograph shows people enjoying the sun and swimming in the Delaware River near the Camden Motorboat Club building and dock at Pyne Poynt. A motor yacht is tied to the club's floating dock. (HSW.)

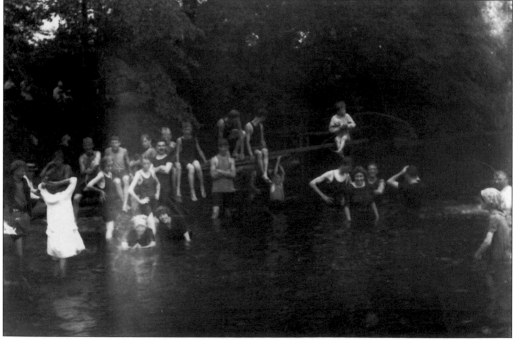

A group cools off in the Cooper River, including five boys seated on two boards on top of a pipe in front of a wooden footbridge. The location is probably a swimming hole where the Edison Park tributary joins the Cooper River in Haddon Township. (CCLS.)

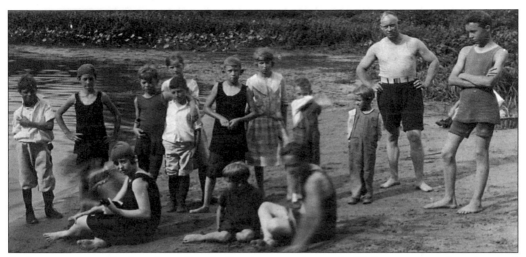

Bathers pose on the beach at Sandy Bend, a popular early-20th-century swimming and boating location on the south shore of the Cooper River in Haddon Township's Westmont neighborhood. (CCLS.)

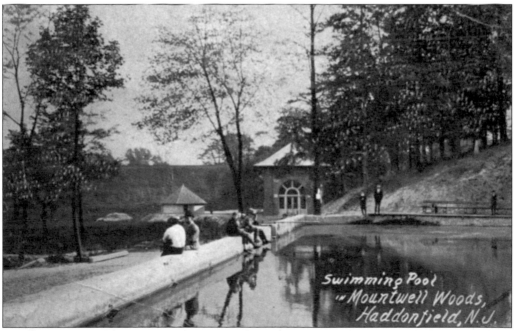

People enjoy the outdoors seated on the wall of the swimming pool in Mountwell Woods, Haddonfield, in this c. 1920s photograph. The concrete pool shown here replaced an earlier pool the Haddonfield Fortnightly civic organization built in 1913. The Haddonfield Fortnightly pool builders cleverly impounded a small stream that flows into the Cooper River with cobblestones removed from pedestrian crossings before Kings Highway was paved. (PS.)

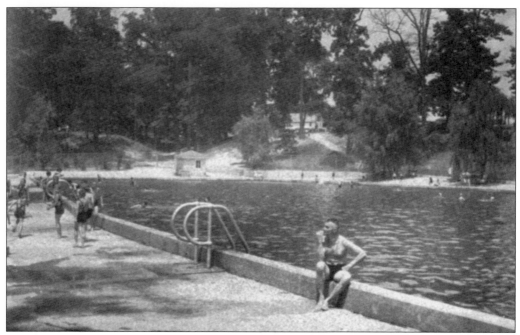

The Camden County Park Commission acquired the Mountwell Pool site in 1928 and later constructed a large concrete pool, seen here around 1937. The pool, once described as "Haddonfield's most popular bathing spot and recreation center," closed in 1973 because of structural problems and because storm water had begun to wash nearby vegetation and mud into the pool, forcing operators to frequently empty and close it. (CCHS.)

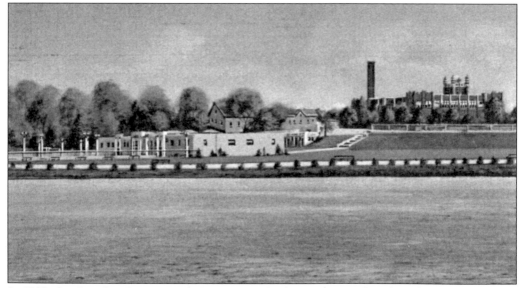

In 1929, the Camden County Park Commission built a county park within the city of Camden on 33 acres of marsh and highland east of Pine Street. The New Camden Park, which opened on May 30, 1931, included tennis courts, a bathhouse (seen here to the left of Camden High School), and one of the largest swimming-pool complexes in the United States. The park included athletic fields, an open-air dance floor, a bandstand, and playgrounds. The park entrances were located on Park and Baird Boulevards at the base of Red Hill. (PS.)

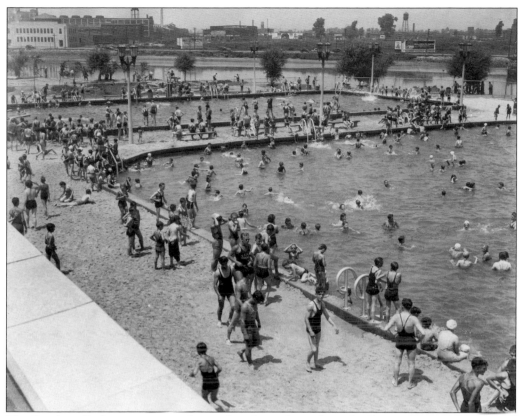

The Farnham Park swimming pool complex, shown here along the Cooper River with Admiral Wilson Boulevard and industrial buildings in the background, included diving, racing, and wading pools. The complex served 5,000 people on a hot day in 1933 and 145,000 in 1936's swimming season. The county designated the Farnham Park pools for whites only. The park commission demolished the pool and the bathhouse 30 years later, leaving only the baseball field and tennis courts. (CCHS.)

This is a view facing southwest of the approach and northeast entrance to the New Camden Park and swimming pool complex from Baird Boulevard Bridge. The stone retaining walls along the South Bank of the Cooper River and along the lower slope of Red Hill remain today. The former auto roadway entrance from Baird Boulevard has been converted into a Camden Greenway pedestrian path. (CCPC.)

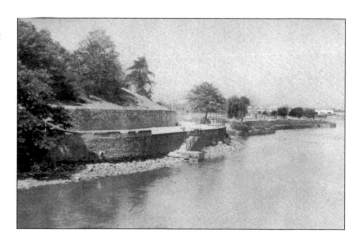

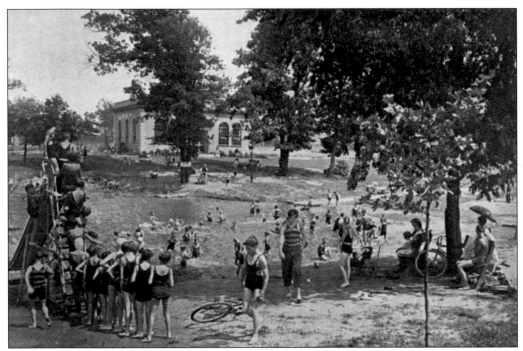

The WPA built Robert's Park and Pool in Collingswood in the 1930s. Here, bathers line up to use the lake slide. The park pump house is in the background. (CCC&HC.)

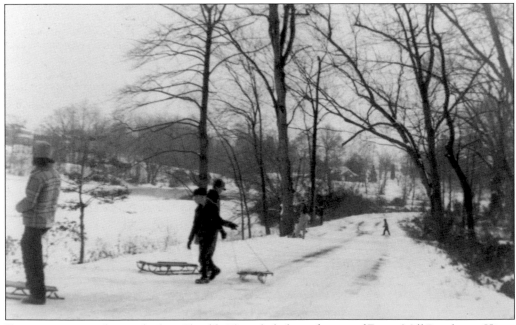

Youngsters get ready to ride their Flexible Flyer sleds from the top of Evans Mill Road near Kings Highway in Haddonfield. Their path will take them toward the Evans Pond Dam, visible right of center. Wallworth Lake (left) and clubhouse (center) are seen in the photograph. (HSH.)

Six

BRIDGES, BOULEVARD, AND AIRPORT

The automobile profoundly altered Camden County's economy and landscape, especially along the Cooper River corridor. Its explosive growth increased demand for new and vastly upgraded bridges and highways, shifted business locations and development outside the city, and led to new ways to think about and design public places and parks.

This chapter shows how the river's bridges and roads evolved in response to changing transportation needs and how those changes affected the location and types of new businesses. Admiral Wilson (Route 30) and Crescent (Route 130) Boulevards had perhaps the most impact on Camden and its suburbs, as the first was designed to speed motorists quickly through, and the second to route them completely around, the city of Camden. Named for Adm. Henry Braid Wilson Jr., a Camden native and World War I naval hero, Admiral Wilson Boulevard has been the most famous and, alternately, the most infamous road in South Jersey. When originally conceived, the boulevard was meant to be a tree-lined parkway, providing motorists with pleasant views of the river, Camden High School, and city- and county-owned parks along the Cooper River. State highway officials abandoned this idea when they decided to sell the land adjacent to the boulevard to private interests rather than turn it over to the city for parks.

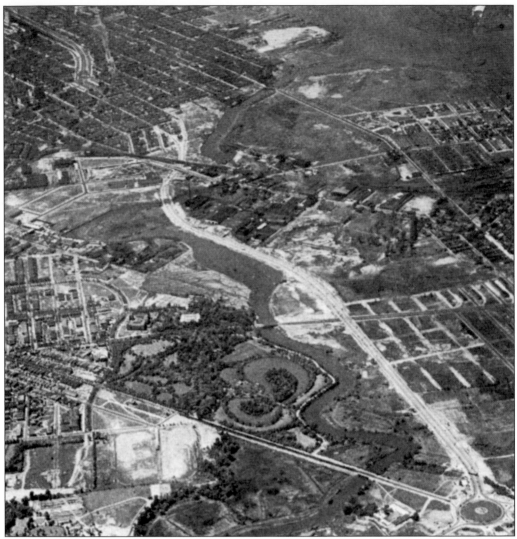

The Cooper River flows almost parallel to Admiral Wilson Boulevard (Route 30) in this c. 1930 photograph. The river runs from the bottom center of the photograph, left of the Airport Circle, to its confluence with the Delaware River at the center top. Admiral Wilson Boulevard runs from the Airport Circle on the lower right, proceeding west along the Cooper River's right bank, crossing it just east of the Sears Building. The boulevard then proceeds through the city of Camden on two local streets before reaching the Ben Franklin Bridge (upper left). (LCP.)

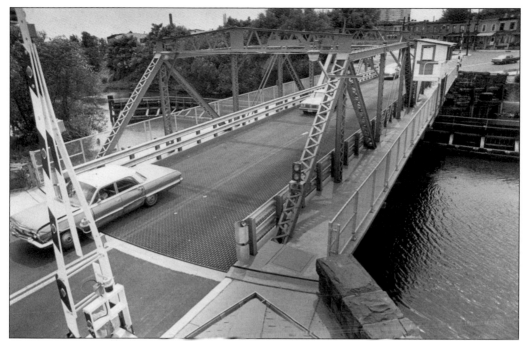

The first bridge across the Cooper River closest to its confluence with the Delaware River is the State Street Bridge. Daniel Bishop built a bridge in this location in 1857. Benjamin Sweeten erected a Warren through truss, center-pivot bridge in 1899 to replace it. Camden County built a fixed replacement bridge in 2013 and converted the bridge seen in this June 1977 photograph for pedestrian use. (SCRCTUL.)

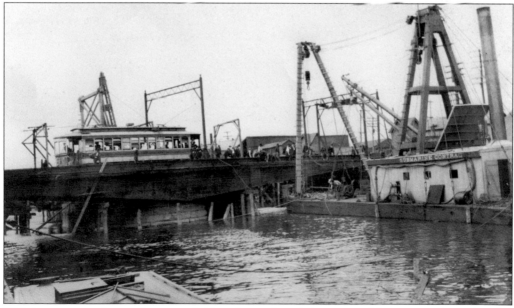

This iron center-pivot swing-span bridge, shown here being crossed by a streetcar, replaced a town-truss covered bridge that was built to cross the Cooper River at Spicer's Ferry (today's Federal Street Bridge) in 1868. The Camden Iron Works required riverboats to be no wider than 16 feet in order to pass between the pivot and the shore. (CCHS.)

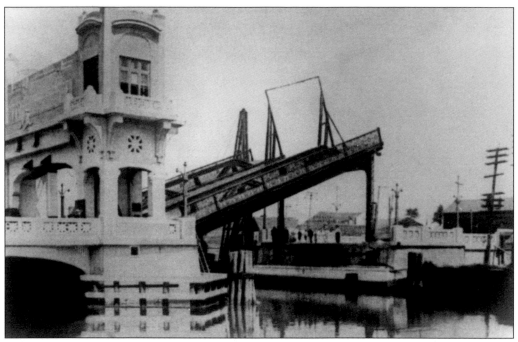

Thomas Spicer established a ferry across Cooper's Creek and a tavern on the eastern bank in 1736, near today's Federal Street Bridge (shown here in an open position). While Haddonfield opposed constructing a bridge here on the grounds that it would block navigation and divert commerce, proponents went ahead and built a bridge at Spicer's Crossing in 1762 to make travel to Cooper's Ferry more convenient along the Burlington Road. Gen. George Washington ordered the bridge destroyed in early 1778 to impede British soldiers. The present single-leaf bascule span (pictured), built by Sherzer Rolling Bridge in 1908, replaced an 1868 iron center-pivot bridge. The City of Camden rehabilitated, strengthened, and permanently pinned the bridge shut in the early 1990s. (CCHS.)

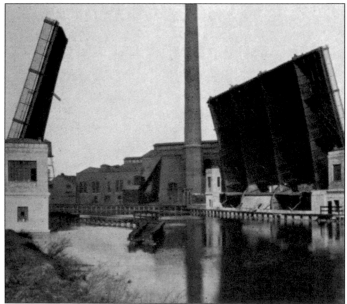

In 1927, M. Straub & Koslyn Company built the double-leaf bascule drawbridge shown here to allow Admiral Wilson Boulevard to cross the Cooper River. The Public Service Railway built the electric generation station located behind the bridge in 1907 to provide power to its electric streetcar operations in the greater Camden area. Public Service demolished the station during the Depression. The New Jersey Department of Transportation replaced the drawbridge with a fixed bridge in 1998. (CCHS.)

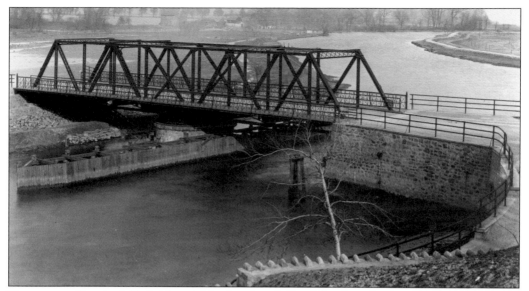

To connect Camden's Parkside neighborhood with Baird Boulevard, county contractor Aaron Ward built a Warren truss center-pivot swing bridge, shown here in 1903. The Hatch Farm and barns can been seen in the background. The embankment separating Forest Hill Park's lake from the river is visible on the upper right. A road with side railings was the north entrance to New Camden Park. This bridge remained in service until 1948, when the state and Camden County constructed a cloverleaf intersection between Baird and Admiral Wilson Boulevards and replaced this bridge with a fixed span. (CCHS.)

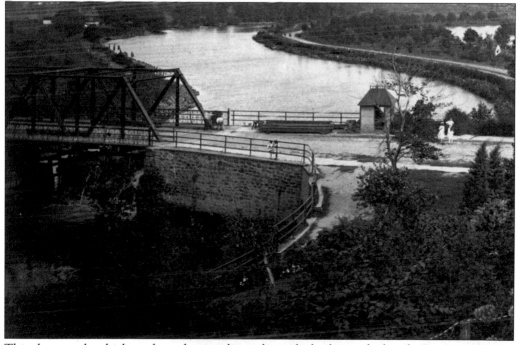

This photograph, which predates the one above, shows the bridge tender booth. Operators inspect the bridge's swing joint, and two girls overlook the bridge abutment rail. At right, three girls stand on Baird Boulevard south of the keeper's kiosk. (CCHS.)

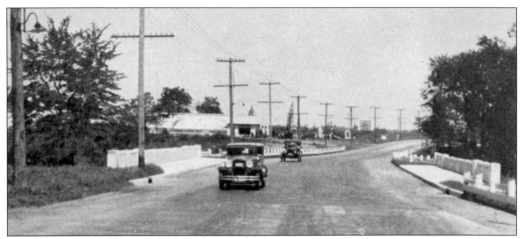

Automobiles approach Haddonfield from Delaware Township (now Cherry Hill) across the Grove Street Bridge in the 1930s. A Works Progress Administration (WPA) greenhouse, later converted to a garden store, is behind the first car in the center distance. County engineer B.M. Schumucker designed the bridge in 1931. (CCHS.)

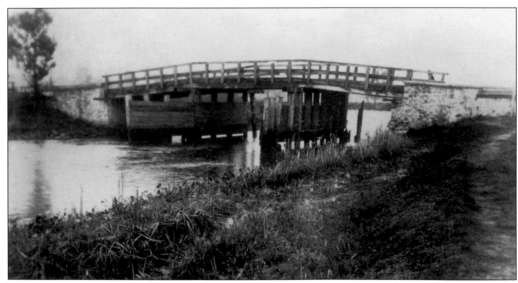

The Browning Road Bridge was similar to other 19th-century country bridges crossing the Cooper River for horse and wagon use. This arched wooden span, about 60 feet long, stood nine feet above the river. (HSH.)

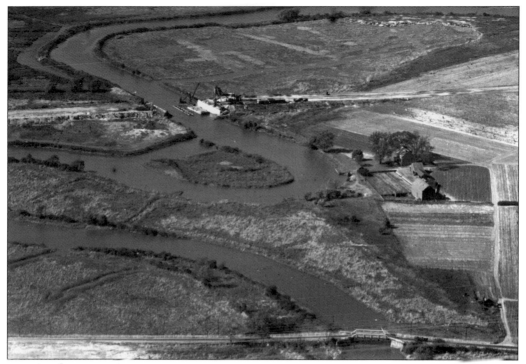

Camden County replaced the Browning Road Bridge with a flat truss bridge, seen at lower right in this 1926 photograph. The Crescent Boulevard Bridge, shown under construction at upper center, was built by the New Jersey State Highway Department as part of the Camden Extension project. All of the river's banks east and west of the Crescent Boulevard Bridge and the Browning Road Bridge were dredged away in the late 1930s to create Cooper River Lake. (CB.)

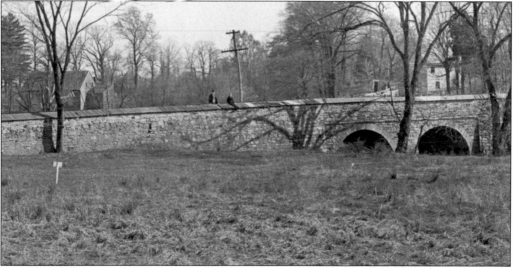

The double-arched stonemasonry Kings Highway Bridge, shown here around 1910, was replaced with a single-arched bridge in 1915. Samuel Nicholson Rhoads and his son Evan (sitting on the bridge rail) face northwest across a floodplain on the Delaware (Cherry Hill) Township side of the bridge. The Evans Mill building and Croft Farm barn are visible on the left, and the miller's house with outdoor privy can be seen at right. (HSH.)

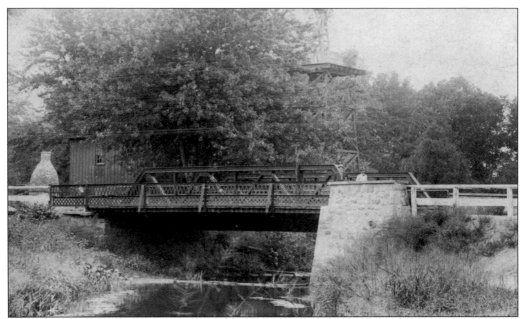

This iron-truss bridge crossed the Cooper River between Potter Street and Batesville near the location of the intersection of the Haddonfield-Berlin and Kresson Roads. The Rustic Terra Cotta Works building was to the left of this bridge, behind the large "bottle-shaped" pot. A windmill tower is visible behind the two men on the bridge on the Haddonfield side of the Cooper River. This photograph was taken in the 1920s. (HSH.)

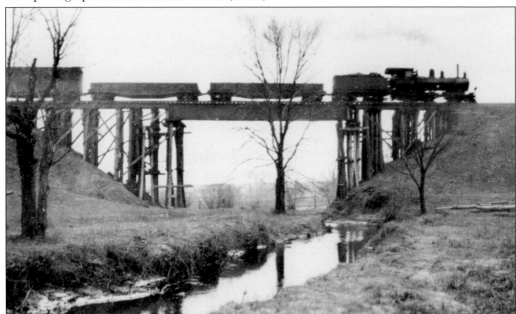

The Philadelphia-Marlton-Medford Railroad Bridge crossed the Cooper River on a trestle near Mountwell, just south of the Haddonfield waterworks, as shown in this March 1913 photograph taken by Charles Z. Vaughan. Passenger service on this line stopped in 1927, and the line was removed from service in 1932. The station near Covered Bridge and Kresson Roads was called Orchard, and the station near Uxbridge was named Freeman. (CCHS.)

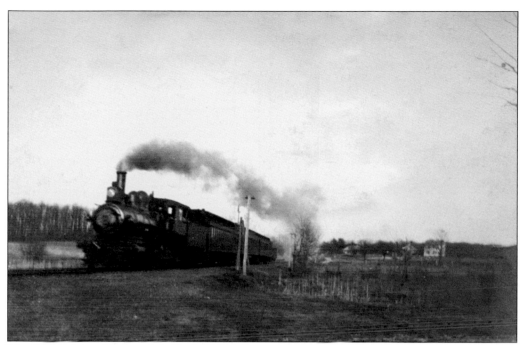

The Philadelphia-Marlton-Medford (PM&M) train shown in this November 1909 photograph in the vicinity of the Orchard station (near the intersection of Kresson and Covered Bridge Roads in Cherry Hill) trails smoke from its coal-burning steam engine as it pulls three passenger cars. The PM&M merged with other railroads in 1896 and became the Medford Branch of the West Jersey & Seashore Railroad controlled by the Pennsylvania Railroad. (CB.)

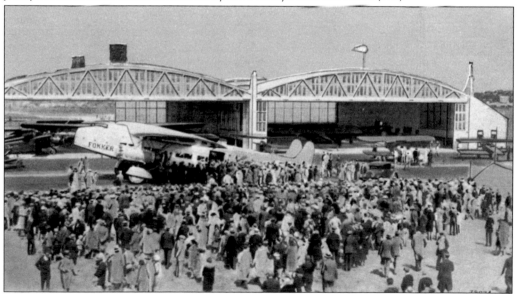

Nicholas Ludington and P. Townsend built the Camden Central Airport on 225 barren acres north of the Cooper River in Pennsauken in 1929. The airport and hangers served Eastern Air Transport, Luddington Flying Service, Curtiss-Wright Flying Services, and Transcontinental and Western Airlines. In this c. 1932 postcard, a crowd of people inspects a 32-pasenger Fokker F.32 aircraft. (PS.)

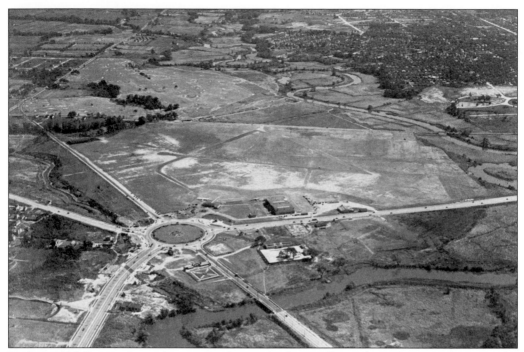

Built in 1925, Pennsauken's Airport Circle was the first traffic circle in the United States. The circle connected Route 30 (Admiral Wilson Boulevard, headed toward the lower left) with Route 130 (passing across the middle of the photograph), Route 38 (upper left), and Kaighn Avenue (going toward the lower right and crossing the Cooper River). Camden's U-drive "Whoopee" car roller coaster is at lower left, on the north side of Admiral Wilson Boulevard. (CCHS.)

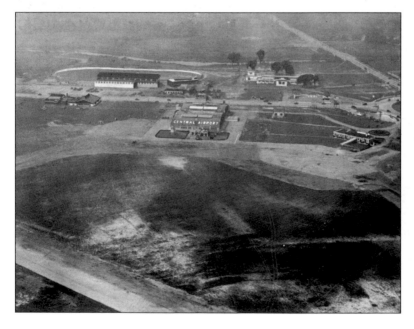

Camden's Central Airport main terminal was located on the east side of Route 130 across from the Pennsauken Kennell Club greyhound dog track built in 1934. Kaighn Avenue crosses the Cooper River west of the airport in the upper right side. (CCHS.)

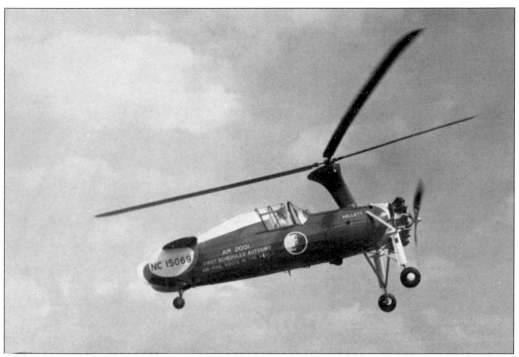

The Camden Airport received airmail for Philadelphia starting in 1929. It was initially driven to the Philadelphia Post Office until the Eastern Air Lines Kellett KD-1B autogiro, seen here around 1930, proved it could ferry the mail faster than trucks by landing on the downtown post office roof in 1939, instituting the first scheduled autogiro airmail route in the world. (CB.)

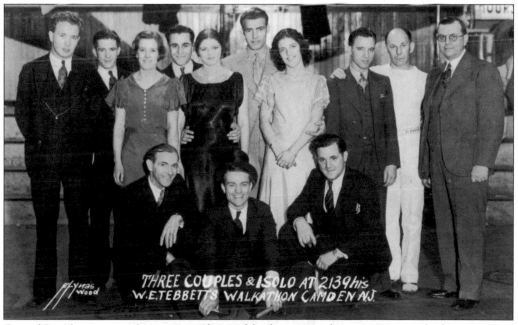

One of Camden Airport's hangars was also used for dance marathons, contests in which participants attempted to dance the longest. Comedian Red Skelton, seated at center with a top hat, was the master of ceremonies at one of W.E. Tebbett's Walkathons at the airport in 1933. (PS.)

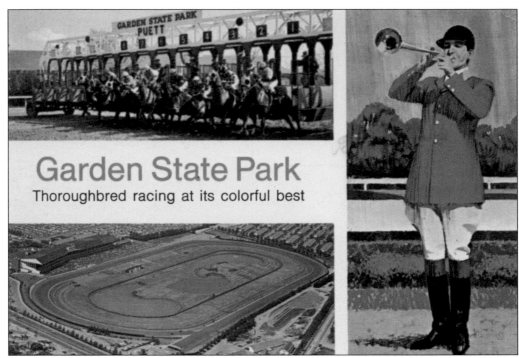

Garden State Park
Thoroughbred racing at its colorful best

Cherry Hill's Garden State Park horse-racing track opened in July 1942 northwest of the intersection of the Marlton Pike and Haddonfield Road, north of the Cooper River's Grove Street Bridge. Fire heavily damaged the racetrack buildings in 1977. The racetrack attracted a number of high-end hotels, restaurants, and nightclubs, including the Hawaiian Cottage, Cinelli's Country House, the Rickshaw Inn, the Cherry Hill Inn, and the Latin Casino restaurant theater, which opened in 1960. Entertainers such as Frank Sinatra, Dean Martin, the Supremes, and Liberace performed at the Latin Casino, which closed in 1978 because of competition from the shows at gambling casinos in Atlantic City. (PS.)

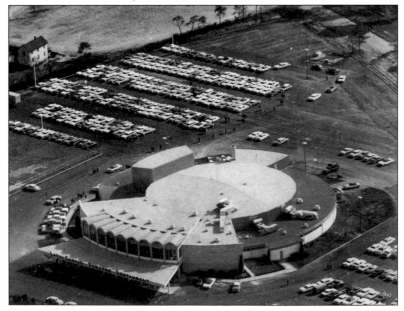

This aerial photograph of the Latin Casino offers an interesting juxtaposition of the modern and the historic. (CHHC.)

Seven

THE PARKWAY PLAN AND MUNN'S MEADOW PARK

Munn's Meadow Park was the first park Charles Wellford Leavitt Jr. designed and built for the Camden County Park Commission and the first the commission built. Leavitt designed the park in October 1927, the same month the parks commission hired him. The commission dredged the meadow and wetlands to form a lake connected with the overflowing Evans Pond and built a Colonial-style recreation building and tennis courts. Leavitt's contract was short-lived. The commission justified ending his contract because it already had "sufficient data . . . to substantially carry through its program." Eldridge Johnson, disturbed about Leavitt's termination, wrote to commission president Wallworth: "A story has reached me that the so-called Republican leader [David Baird Sr.] has offered to impose his dead body between Leavitt and the park enterprise. Well, he is working on the right lines; there is no more certain way to commit political suicide than to obstruct the completion of the Camden parks." Johnson also wrote that the commission "should never have been allowed to come under the control of the political element . . . who do not have the true interests of the city at heart, but who organize themselves into a gang for personal gain." (The letters quoted are in the Johnson Victrola Museum collection.)

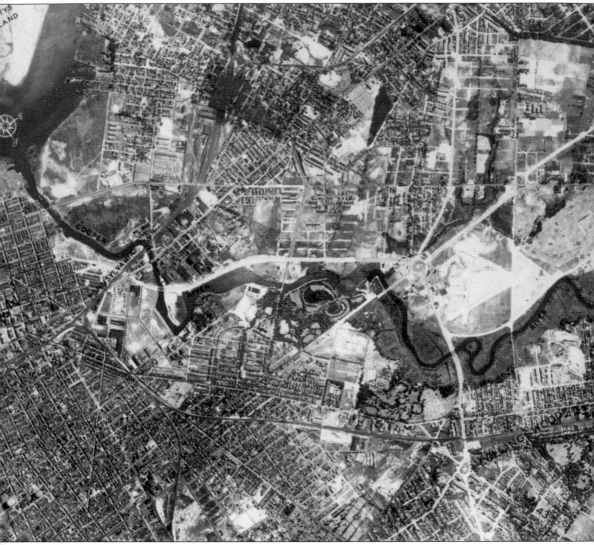

This c. 1930 photograph shows the meandering path of the Cooper River from the Haddonfield railroad bridge (lower right) to its confluence with the Delaware River (top left), below Petty's Island. Camden's Central Airport and Airport Circle are in the center, to the left of the Cooper Valley Country Club Golf Course, whose sand traps are visible above the Cooper's largest oxbow bend east of the airport. Farnham Park's dog-bone-shaped lake and island, west of Airport Circle,

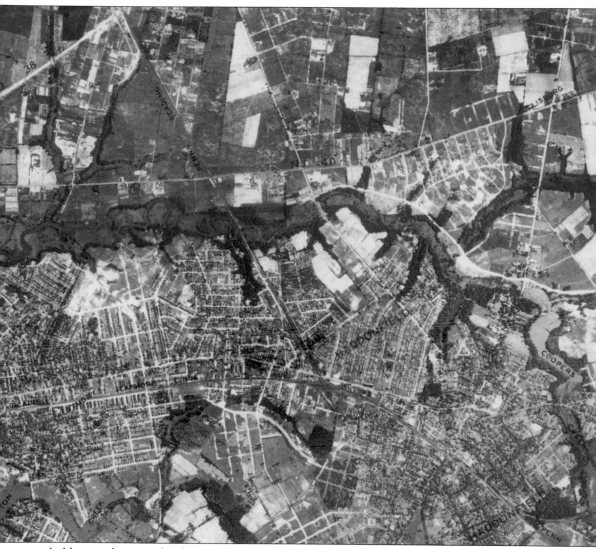

are held intact by an embankment along the Cooper's left (southern) bank, and New Camden Park's swimming pool complex is visible west of the Baird Boulevard Bridge. (This map was prepared using NJDEP Bureau of GIS digital data, but this secondary product has not been verified by NJDEP and is not state authorized.)

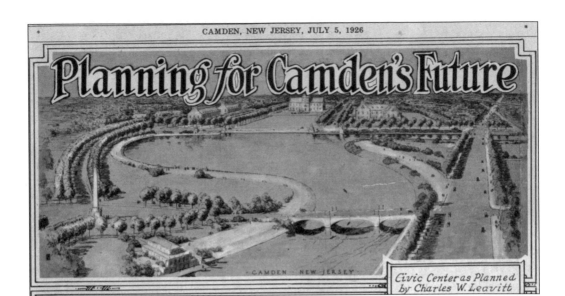

Planning for Camden's Future

·CAMDEN·NEW·JERSEY·

Civic Center as Planned by Charles W. Leavitt

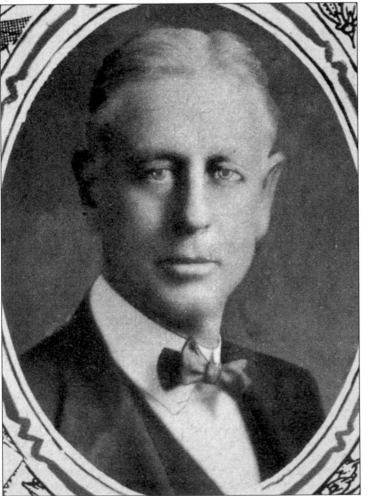

In 1923, Camden mayor Victor King recruited urban planning expert Charles W. Leavitt Jr. of New York to develop a city growth plan in light of impending increases in automobile traffic anticipated by the construction of the first bridge between Philadelphia and Camden. As suggested in the *Courier Post*'s 1926 headline (above), Leavitt not only drew up elaborate blueprints for a parkway and a multilane expressway from the city line to the bridge, he also prepared a regional plan that included a new Camden City civic center overlooking the Cooper River, where Campbell Soup's corporate headquarters are today. Leavitt (left) was called a "rare combination of engineer, artist, and diplomat" by New York newspaper publisher David Stone. (CB.)

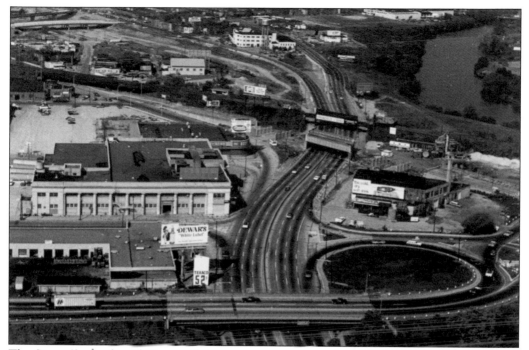

The Sears, Roebuck and Co. retail department store opened in July 1927 on Admiral Wilson Boulevard, west of the Cooper River. It operated until September 1971. The Sears building and the Admiral Wilson Boulevard bridge were the only structures built according to Classical Revival architectural standards prescribed by Leavitt for the Camden civic center area. It was demolished in 2013. (CCHS.)

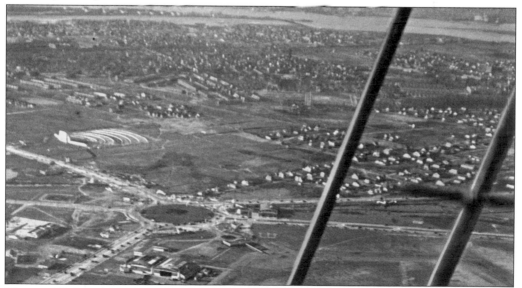

The world's first drive-in movie theater (on the left in the photograph) opened on Admiral Wilson Boulevard in 1933. Richard Hollingshead Jr. invented the drive-in because his mother disliked squeezing into movie theater seats. *Wives Beware*, the theater's first movie, was projected onto a 40-by-50-foot screen and heard through three 36-square-foot speakers provided by RCA Victor. (CCHS.)

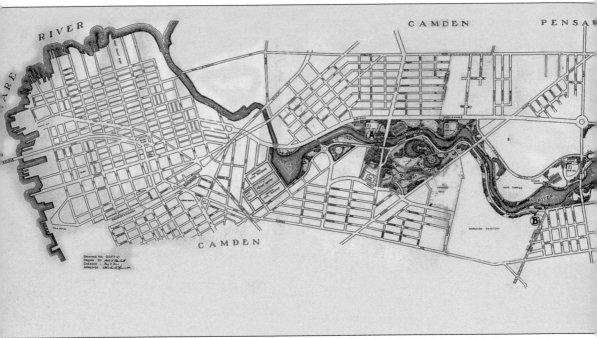

The importance Leavitt placed on the details of design is evident in his 1925 Cooper River Parkway plan, which defines every recreation area and its purpose. He designed the plan to enhance and fit a preexisting natural waterway. He believed that "Nature dominates the world. Man must design his work to fit in with nature, not try to fit nature to his needs." Leavitt's plan embodies the work of landscape architect Frederick Law Olmsted (designer of New York City's Central Park), who believed that there is no beauty without utility. Rather than aim merely for

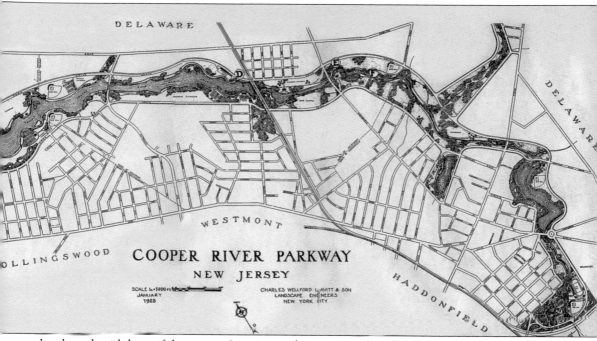

DELAWARE

DELAWARE

WESTMONT

COLLINGSWOOD

COOPER RIVER PARKWAY
NEW JERSEY

SCALE 1 = 1400 ft
JANUARY
1928

CHARLES WELLFORD LEAVITT & SON
LANDSCAPE ENGINEERS
NEW YORK CITY

HADDONFIELD

a lovely park with beautiful greenery, Leavitt sought to create a healthy environment to promote democracy by incorporating democratic and egalitarian principles in his designs. Like Olmsted's park designs, Leavitt's Cooper River Park plan is centered on water and includes both wooded and open spaces; informal, naturalistic landscaping; storm-water management; footpath systems; drives meandering through the parks and directing vehicular traffic flow away from urban streets; scenic views; pedestrian bridges over waterways; and far-ranging vistas. (HSW.)

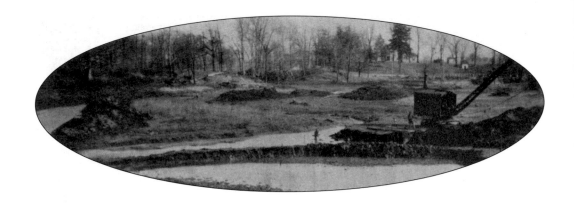

These 1928 photographs show Munn's Meadow before and after the Camden County Park Commission completed Leavitt's 1927 plans. The concrete and riverstone-faced dam shown below is on the northwest border of Wallworth Lake, about 150 feet east of the Kings Highway Bridge. The park commission built it in the location designated on Leavitt's October 1927 Munn's Meadow Park Landscape Plan. Munn's Meadow Park—the name of which was changed to Wallworth Park following the 1933 reported suicide of the park commission's first president, Sen. Joseph Wallworth—was the first park that the CCPC built in the Cooper River Park system. (Above, CB; below, PS.)

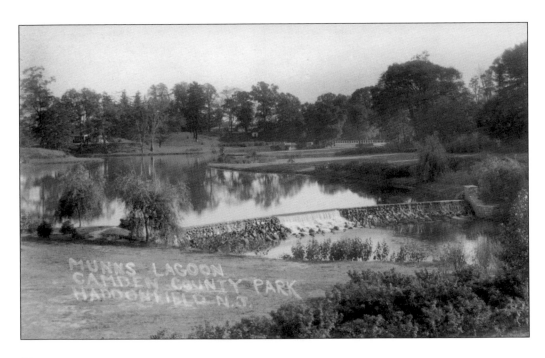

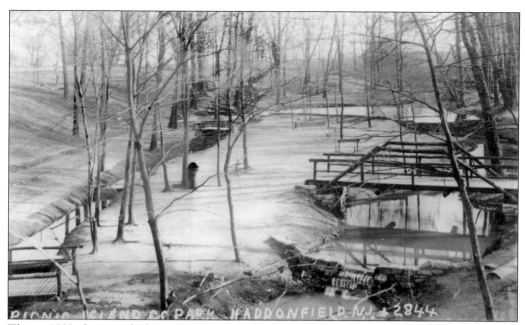

This c. 1929 photograph shows "Picnic Park Island" in Wallworth Park along Buckman's Run, a Cooper River tributary that flows westward under Caldwell Road from a spring-fed pond in the Hunt Tract in Cherry Hill to Wallworth Lake. As seen here, the park commission created an artificial island in Buckman's Run south of Park Boulevard by digging a channel on the "island's" north side. The photograph shows several impoundments and three wooden footbridges to the island. None of these exist today. (HSH.)

Ice-skaters enjoy frozen Wallworth Lake. The photograph, taken around 1930 from the Kings Highway Bridge, shows a footbridge over the Cooper River between the riverstone Wallworth Lake dam and Kings Highway, and a parking lot on the bank above the lake. (CCPC.)

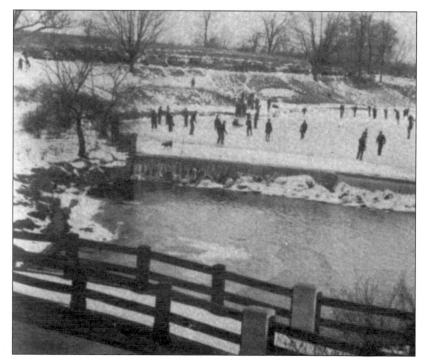

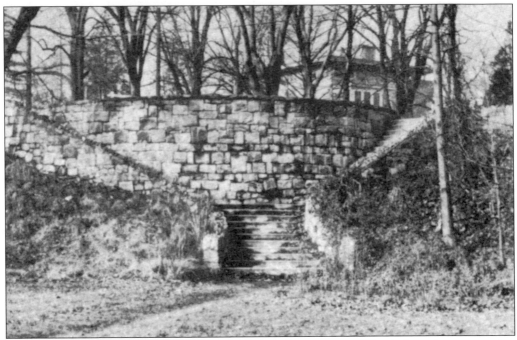

This WPA-era Pennsylvania mica stone staircase and retaining wall leads from the intersection of Kings Highway and Evans Mill Road down to Wallworth Park. The park commission published this photograph in a 1937 progress report. (CCPC.)

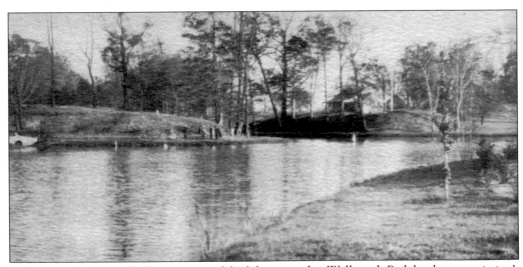

This c. 1937 photograph shows a view of the lake created at Wallworth Park by the commission's dam. A stone footbridge is on the far left side and Wallworth Clubhouse, the park's only building, right of center, overlooks Buckman's Run and the lake. The Evans Pond Dam is to the right, beyond the frame of the photograph. (CCPC.)

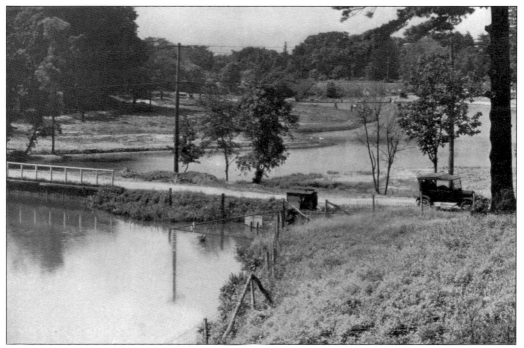

This c. 1923 photograph shows Evans Pond in the left foreground and Wallworth Lake behind the Evans Pond Dam. This view faces northwest from the Croft Farm House to Haddonfield and the Kings Highway Bridge in the distance. (HSW.)

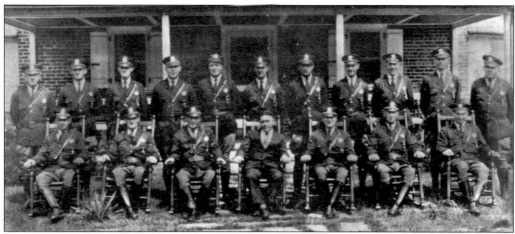

The first Camden County Park Commission police force poses in front of the Wallworth Clubhouse around 1929. The clubhouse was used as a headquarters and meeting place. The park police were absorbed into the newly formed Camden County Police Department in 2013. (CCPC.)

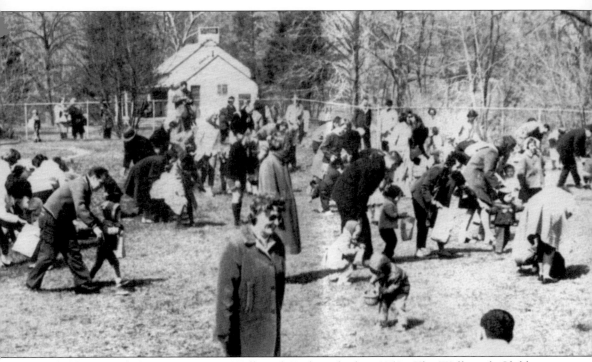

Children search for Easter eggs in Wallworth Park in the late 1950s. The Wallworth Clubhouse is visible in the background. (HSH.)

Eight

PENNYPACKER PARK AND THE CIVILIAN CONSERVATION CORPS

More than 200 Civilian Conservation Corps (CCC) boys, stationed at nearby Camp Cooper, built Pennypacker Park between Grove Street and Kings Highway beginning in 1934. Named in honor of James Lane Pennypacker, Haddonfield historian, botanist, and poet, the park area was cleared and thinned, replanted with acres of deciduous trees and shrubbery native to New Jersey, and equipped with footpaths and bridges. The CCC also dredged thousands of cubic yards of mud and earth to create Grove Lake from the river. Pennypacker Park is adjacent to Hopkins Pond and Birdwood, one of Haddonfield's most historic homes. As recounted on page 32, William Foulke made Birdwood famous for his recognition that an unusually large bone that the Hopkins family had kept as a curio for 20 years probably belonged to a dinosaur. Foulke and scientist Joseph Leidy dug up the rest of the bones in a marl pit at the end of Maple Avenue. Leidy assembled the world's first almost fully intact dinosaur from the bones. As a result, the site of the find is a National Historic Landmark in Pennypacker Park and is listed in the National Register of Historic Places.

James Lane Pennypacker's 1896 poem "Down Cooper's Creek" paints a kinetic river rich in trees, flowers, and animal life:

> Do you know
> How the waters go
> Down Cooper's Creek?
> Tumbling o'er the ridges,
> Cutting through the sand,
> Whirling under bridges,
> Eating out the land,
> Through the meadow reaches
> Swinging left and right,
> By the rooted beeches
> Pools as black as night
> Lingering long in the marshes, green and quiet and wide,
> Await and ready to welcome the slow incoming tide.

Have you seen
The dark ravine
Down Cooper's Creek?
Oaks and burning bushes,
Dogwood trees and pines,
Ferns and brakes and rushes,
Grape and smilax vines,
Bloodroot, jacks and mallows,
Windflowers on the bank,
And filling all the hollows
Cabbage wild and rank,
And a jungle of climbing and creeping things with their lights and
shades,
That sweeps one away with the sense of Florida everglades.

Have you heard
The call of bird
Down Cooper's Creek?
The noisy quarrels
Of the squirrels
Down Cooper's Creek?
Blackbirds and thrushes,
Warblers, chats and jays,
The fisher's rattling rushes
Across the water ways—
The cardinal aflaming,
The chattering little wren,
And the crow aloft proclaiming
His scorn of common men—
And down in the cool of the shadows the fishes silently swim,
And the muskrat lies by bank and as silently watches them.

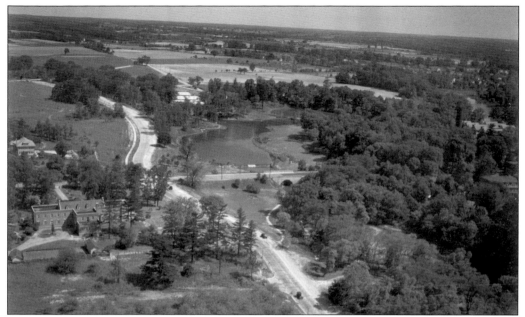

This aerial photograph shows the Kings Highway Bridge and Wallworth Park dam across the Cooper River (right) and the Sheperd's Home at left. Kings Highway is the northern boundary of Pennypacker Park. Wallworth Park tennis courts are visible as white squares beyond Wallworth Lake. Park Boulevard goes from the lower right to the upper left, where it intersects with Caldwell Road. (ISM.)

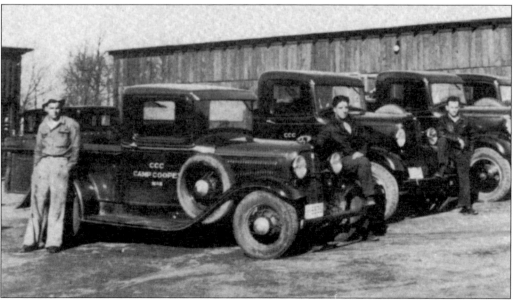

CCC Camp Cooper drivers and their pickup trucks are seen around 1933 at camp buildings located along the Cooper River, northwest of Haddonfield. CCC camps were temporary communities housing up to 200 civilian enrollees (typically unmarried, unemployed males, 18–25 years old, whose families were on local relief). Camps included barracks for 50 enrollees each, and medical dispensaries, mess halls, education buildings, lavatories and showers, and motor pool garages. (CCPC.)

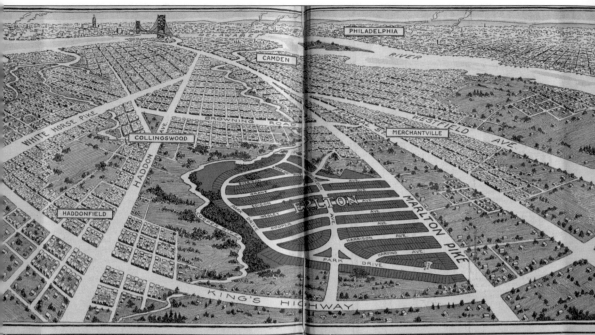

ERLTON *IN THE KINGS HIGHWAY SECTION OF CAMDEN COUNTY*

BY THE BUILDER OF BLUE BIRD HOMES AND HADDONFIELD ESTATES

This 1930s image offers a bird's-eye view of the Cooper River Valley. The map is included in a real estate marketing flyer highlighting the Erlton neighborhood in Delaware Township adjacent to Pennypacker Park between the Cooper River, the Marlton Pike, Browning Road, and Kings Highway. E.R. Lippincott, the builder of the Westmont Blue Bird neighborhood, used his initials for the first three letters of his new development: Erlton. (CB.)

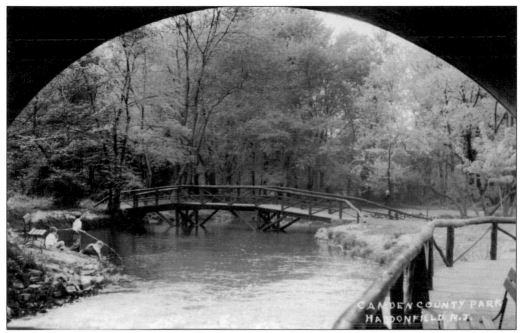

Seen here around 1935, three boys fish the Cooper River at the north end of Pennypacker Park near the Kings Highway Bridge arch and a footbridge to the west. (PS.)

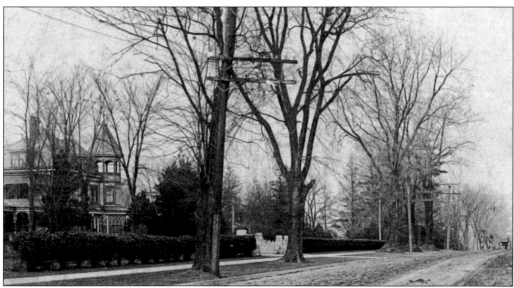

Margaret Bancroft purchased the Lindens, seen here on the left, for her boarding school for handicapped children in 1890. Formerly the home of William Man, its current address is 437 Kings Highway, Haddonfield. Bancroft erected many buildings around the Lindens and elsewhere, becoming the fifth-largest private employer in Camden County today, serving more than 800 children and adults with intellectual and developmental disabilities, autism, and acquired brain injuries. (PS.)

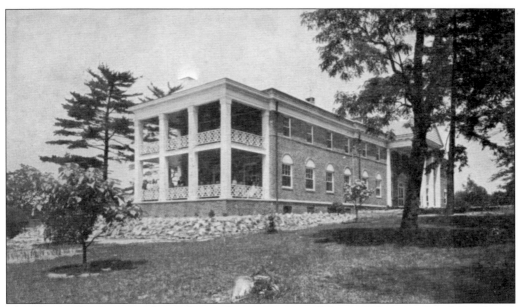

The Shepherds' Home was located near the intersection of Kings Highway and Park Boulevard in Cherry Hill, overlooking the Cooper River. The structure is now an office building. (PS.)

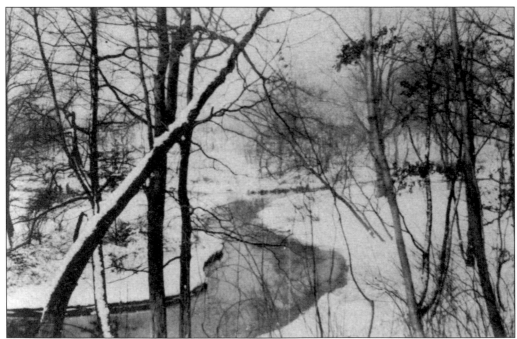

This photograph captures a winter scene along the Cooper River in Pennypacker Park. The woods along the Cooper River in Pennypacker Park look thick and dense with a coat of snow. (CCPC.)

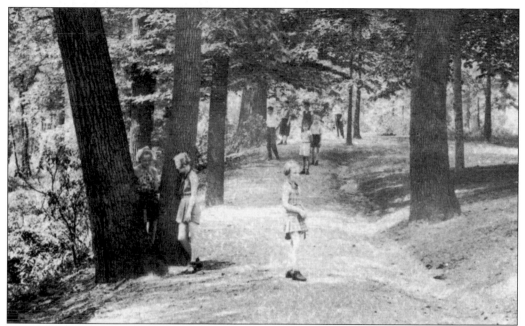

Children stroll along a compacted trail through the forest in Pennypacker Park around 1937. (CCPC.)

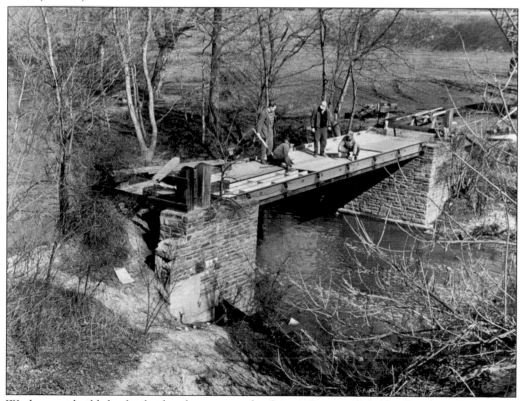

Workmen rebuild the footbridge that crosses the Cooper River in Pennypacker Park connecting Erlton to Hopkins Pond. (SCRCTUL.)

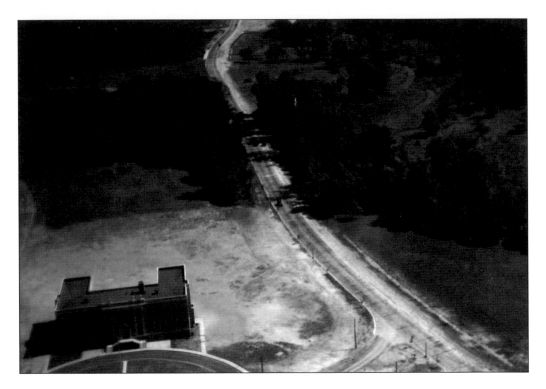

The above photograph, taken around 1928, shows the Erlton School (shortly after it was constructed). The winding Cooper River is on the right. The c. 1962 photograph below offers a front view of the Erlton School after surrounding trees have matured. The Cherry Hill Board of Education closed the school in 1978 due to declining enrollment, and the township demolished the building in 1994. (Above, ISM; below, PS.)

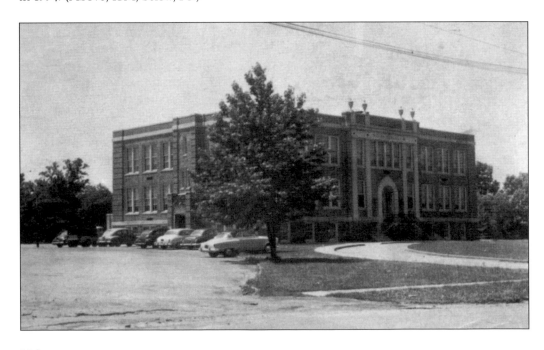

Nine

THE WORKS PROGRESS ADMINISTRATION BUILDS COOPER RIVER LAKE

New Deal agencies provided the manpower and funds to build Cooper River Park in the late 1930s. The Works Progress Administration (renamed in 1939 the Work Projects Administration), the largest and most ambitious New Deal Agency, was the key player in building Cooper River Lake. The WPA's primary mission was to provide jobs to the unemployed during the Great Depression and, in particular, one paid job for all families whose breadwinners suffered long-term unemployment. The WPA provided almost eight million jobs between 1935 and 1943. It employed mostly unskilled men to carry out public works projects, including the construction of buildings, roads, and parks. Almost every community in the United States had a new park, bridge, or school constructed by the agency.

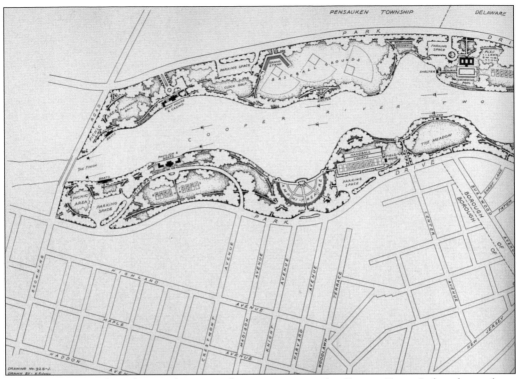

In 1928, Leavitt's firm designed a two-mile rowing course for Cooper River Lake, shown here from Browning Road to Shady Lane. The right half of this drawing appears at the top of page 109. The parks commission described the planned course as two and one half miles long, with an irregular width of from four to nine hundred feet. It said the course would "conform in every respect with the regulations required for International competition. The original purpose of this rowing course was for the pleasure of people who like boating and for high school boys who need practice in preparing to qualify for the boat crews at college. Indications are that trained crews will use the course in competitive races." (HSW.)

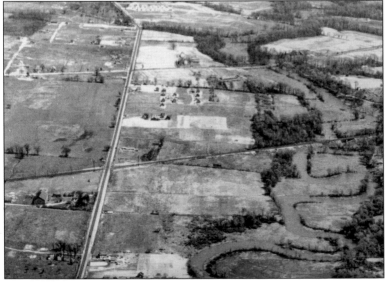

This aerial photograph shows the Cooper River west of the railroad bridge (across the top) and south of the Marlton Pike (running vertically on the left), before Leavitt's dredging and straightening plan was undertaken. (CCHS.)

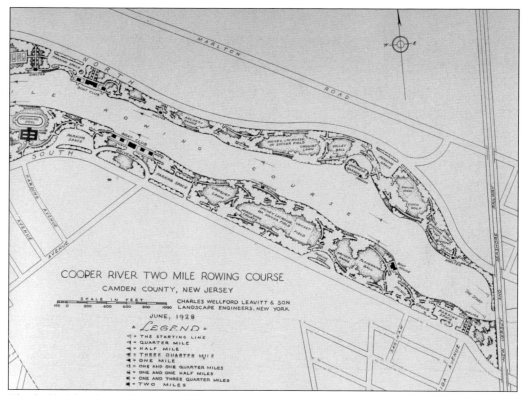

COOPER RIVER TWO MILE ROWING COURSE

CAMDEN COUNTY, NEW JERSEY

SCALE IN FEET
100 0   200   400   600   800   1000

CHARLES WELLFORD LEAVITT & SON
LANDSCAPE ENGINEERS, NEW YORK

JUNE, 1928

• LEGEND •

◁ = THE STARTING LINE
◀ = QUARTER MILE
◀ = HALF MILE
◀ = THREE QUARTER MILE
◀ = ONE MILE
◀◀ = ONE AND ONE QUARTER MILES
◀ = ONE AND ONE HALF MILES
◀ = ONE AND THREE QUARTER MILES
◀ = TWO MILES

This half of the plan for Leavitt's 1928 two-mile rowing course shows its route from Harbor Avenue in Haddon Township to the railroad bridge. Although the location of the course as shown in the design by Leavitt's firm was shifted slightly downstream during its redesign in 1938 (extending to Crescent Boulevard and eliminating the Browning Road Bridge), the course generally has retained its original length and basic shape. (HSW.)

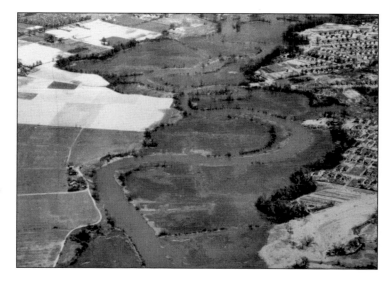

The Cooper River continues its winding path below the section shown on page 108. Westmont's Bluebird neighborhood is on the south side of the Cooper River, at upper right. Collingswood's Cooper River neighborhood is west of (below) Bluebird. (CCHS.)

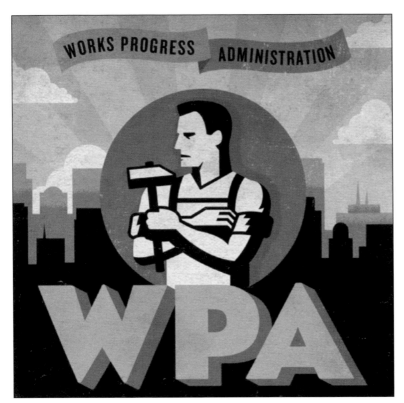

The WPA operated projects in cooperation with state and local governments, which provided 10 to 30 percent of the costs. Usually, the local sponsor provided land and often trucks and supplies, with the WPA responsible for wages (and for the salaries of supervisors, who were not on relief). (CCHS.)

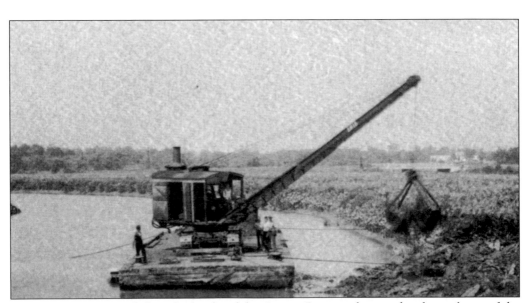

WPA workers blast and clear the banks of the Cooper River to deepen the channel east of the Crescent Boulevard Bridge around 1936. (CCPC.)

This 1938 photograph shows WPA workers constructing Park Drive in the emerging Cooper River Park. A dredge is visible through the thicket, and farmhouses appear on the right. (CCHS.)

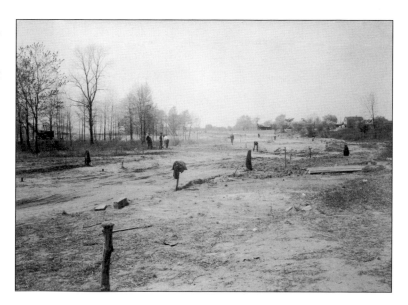

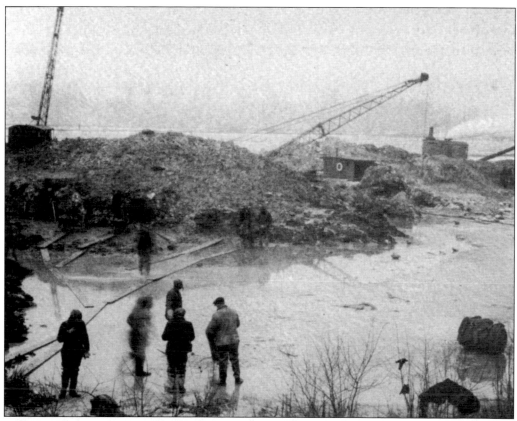

WPA workers operate dredging machines to reshape the Cooper River to create Cooper River Park and Lake between Kaighn Avenue and Crescent Boulevard in February 1936. Cold weather and shifting dredged mud away from the line of dikes made progress difficult. (CCPC.)

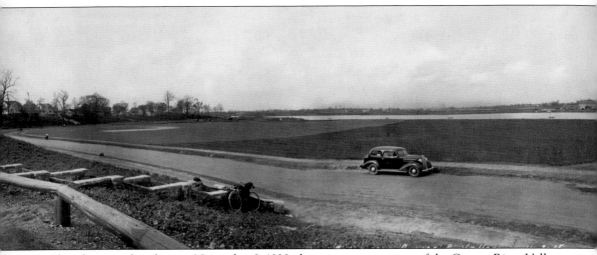

This photograph, taken on November 9, 1938, shows a sweeping view of the Cooper River Valley facing north from South Park Drive in Collingswood. Workers have completed the major dredging and excavation projects to form this part of Cooper River Lake and were engaged in completing south-shore landscaping and South Park Drive roadwork. This north-facing perspective shows an inverted Y-shaped walkway to the lake's south shore and the stone-and-masonry, poured-concrete bleacher benches overlooking an oval track in what would later be named Jack Curtis Stadium on the lake's north shore. The Browning Road Bridge, shown crossing the Cooper River on the far

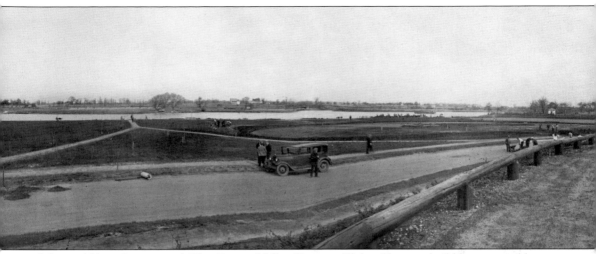

left, would later be removed. The Cooper Valley Country Club golf course buildings are visible to the right of the stadium bleachers on the lake's north shore, as is a dredge spoil barge in the river farther to the right. On the right, three men wearing suits and hats confer in front of a sedan. A fourth man, dressed informally in black and wearing a cap, stands near the car door, holding an unidentifiable object and looking to the southeast. (CCC&HC.)

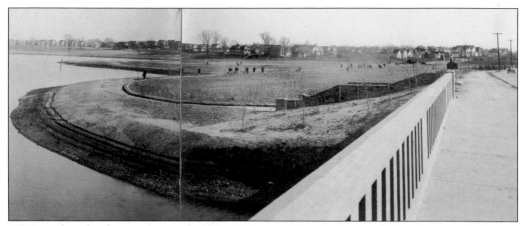

WPA workers landscape the south shore of Cooper River Lake east of the Crescent Boulevard (Route 130) Bridge on March 28, 1938. The photograph was taken from the bridge, with a view facing southeast toward Collingswood and the lake's south shore. A WPA-built Pennsylvania mica stone-and-masonry stairway leads down and to the left from the bridge sidewalk, to a park pathway below. (CCC&HC.)

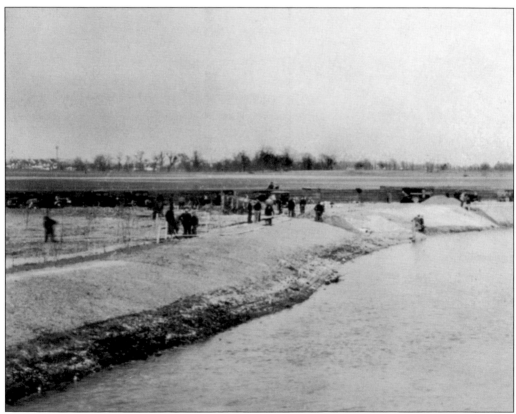

WPA workers landscape the north shore of Cooper River Lake northeast of the Crescent Boulevard (Route 130) Bridge on March 28, 1938. This photograph was taken from the bridge, with a view facing northeast toward Pennsauken and the lake's north shore. Parked in front of a barrier wall are nine black sedans and a small truck. The wall is taller than the sedans. (CCC&HC.)

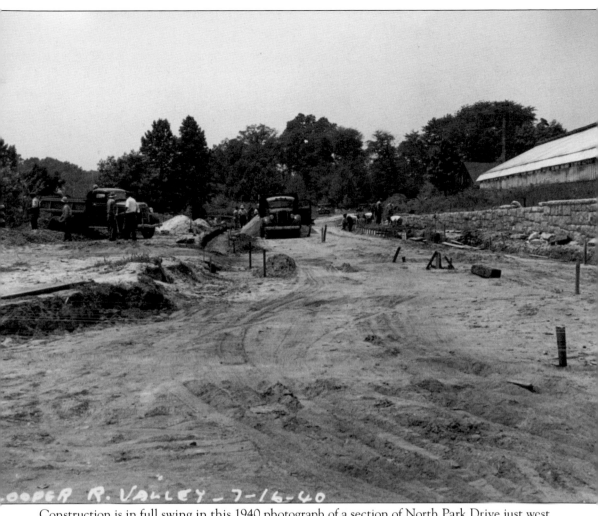

OOPER R. VALLEY – 7-16-40

Construction is in full swing in this 1940 photograph of a section of North Park Drive just west of Pennypacker Park. The WPA had a greenhouse (right) to grow plants destined for the park. The greenhouse site currently houses condominiums and has a modern version of the retaining wall. (CCHS.)

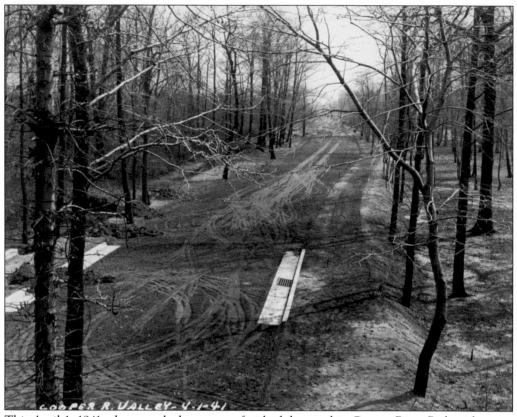

COOPER R. VALLEY- 4-1-41

This April 1, 1941, photograph shows an unfinished dirt road in Cooper River Park with storm drains installed. (CCC&HC.)

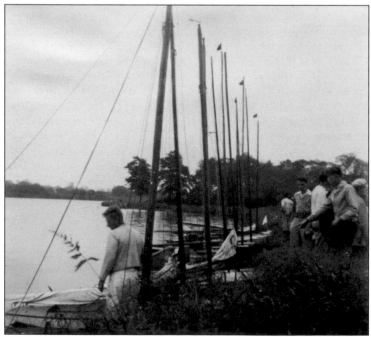

This photograph, entitled *Before We Had a Dock*, was taken from the southern bank of the Cooper River. The Cooper River Yacht Club's founders were a handful of sailing enthusiasts who possessed uncommon foresight. The photograph is dated around 1944. (CRYC.)

Ten

COOPER RIVER PARK

Cooper River Park contains 346.55 acres and extends approximately three miles between South Crescent Boulevard (Pennsauken Township) and Grove Street (Cherry Hill Township) on both sides of Cooper River Lake. Winding vehicular drives, North and South Park Drives, run in an east-west direction generally following the shores of the lake. The park includes the Crescent Avenue and Cuthbert Avenue Bridges, the New Jersey Transit railroad bridge, paved footpaths, paved parking areas, picnic pavilions, stonemasonry features, memorial statues and sculpture, Veterans Island, baseball diamonds, children's playgrounds, a stadium with a quarter-mile running track, and other recreational features described in this chapter. The American Planning Association placed the park on its New Jersey's 2013 "Great Places" list in September 2013, because it is "a sterling illustration of the outcome of good plans and planning, both in its design and development." Camden County freeholder Jeff Nash called the Cooper River Park "the crown jewel of our county park system." Cooper River Lake was central to the park's original design and remains its central feature today. WPA workers created the lake by extensive dredging and filling in and around the Cooper River and the surrounding swampland between 1935 and 1940. The lake extends about 2.4 miles between East Crescent Boulevard on its western end to the eastern end of South Park Drive, where it intersects with Saginaw Avenue in Haddon Township. It is surrounded largely by open parkland and wooded areas between North and South Park Drives and the lake.

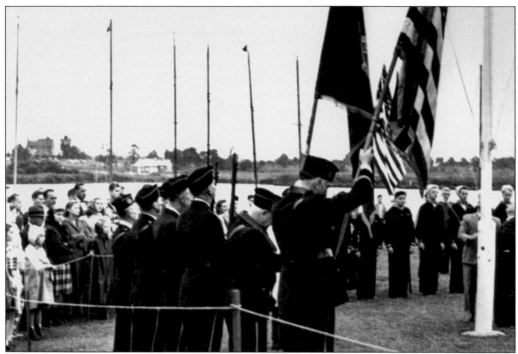

Shown here is the opening-day ceremony of the Cooper River Yacht Club in 1945. Members and their families stand at attention with a color guard of veterans and a half-dozen sea scouts. The Camden County Park Commission donated the club's building by the river and leased the site to the club. CRYC members still volunteer to maintain the clubhouse and grounds. (CRYC.)

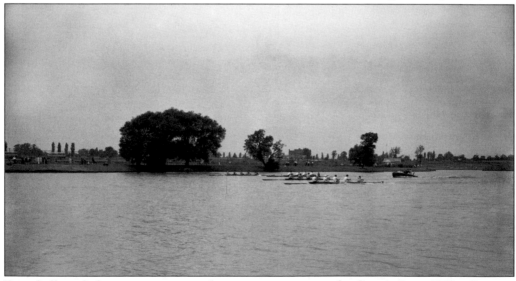

Four shells with four sweep rowers and coxswain power past the Cooper River Valley Country Clubhouse (now the location of the Cooper River Plaza Apartments) and the Camden County Park Commission tennis clubhouse in a Memorial Day Race in 1941. The Cooper River is home to eight area rowing clubs. Numerous major state and national rowing events, including the IRAs, NCAAs, and the SRAA, have chosen the Cooper's sheltered, six-lane, 2,000-meters racecourse for their regattas. (CCLS.)

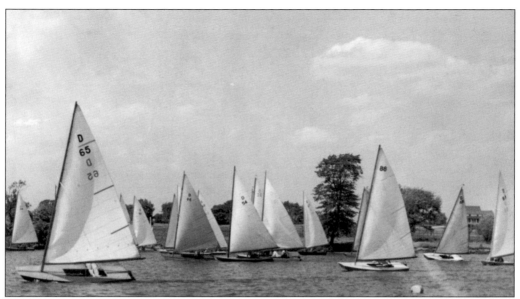

Veteran sailor Harry Chandler from New England started sailboat races at the CRYC. Shown here is a 1947 Duster-class sailboat regatta racing west. The Cooper Valley Country Club golf course building is on the right. The comets below start racing on a tack east, past the Cooper Valley Country Club, in a September 1947 regatta. The Camden County Park Commission building (with a white flagpole), which later became the Lobster Trap and is now the Hadley Building, is on the north shore, at the top right. (Above, CRYC; below, CCLS.)

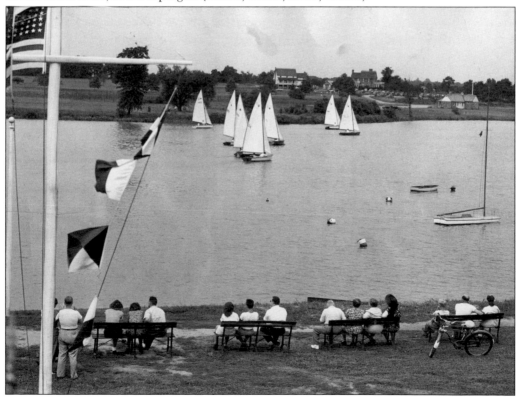

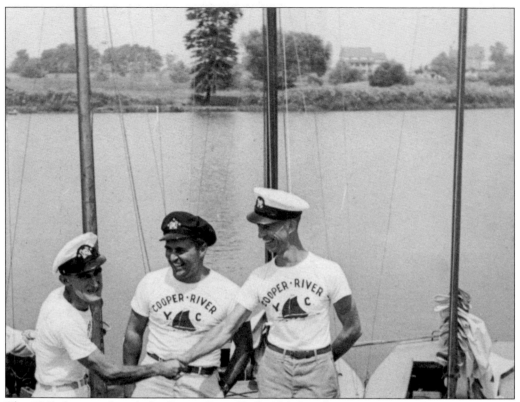

This 1945 photograph includes Cooper River Yacht Club founders Lester B. Hays (left), Commodore J. Leslie Greenfield (center), and Charles Mulford. Also shown are two Cooper Valley Country Club buildings, across the Cooper River to the right. Club sailors have won more than 50 national and international races. Membership remains open to the public. (CRYC.)

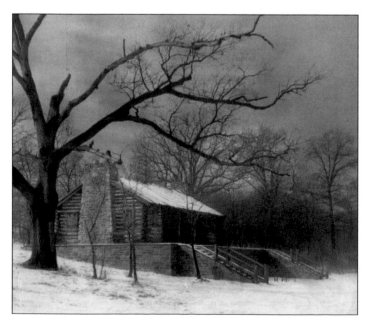

This is the log cabin that once stood along the southern bank of the Cooper River in Haddon Township. The cabin in Saginaw Woods had stairs leading to the river and a fireplace to keep visitors warm. (DR.)

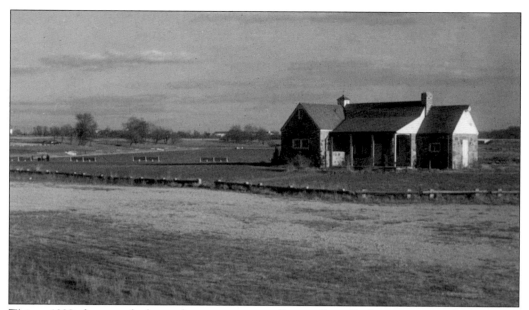

This c. 1939 photograph shows the stonemasonry Cooper River Park tennis court clubhouse on the Cooper River's north shore, adjacent to today's Veterans Memorial Island. Camden County later leased the building to the operators of the Lobster Trap Restaurant, which closed in 2013. The view in the photograph faces east from the clubhouse parking lot. (CCLS.)

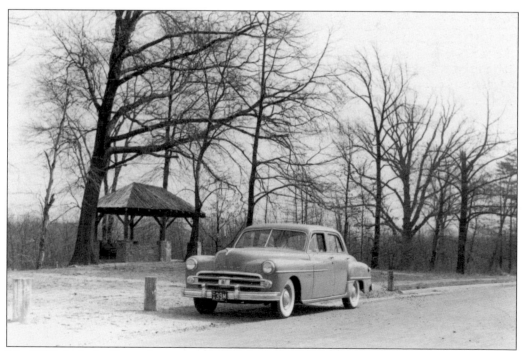

The WPA built the Pennsylvania mica stonemasonry–covered lookout platform and shelter seen in this late-1930s photograph. Before the park's trees matured, this shelter would have provided commanding views up and down the Cooper River near the start of the 2.5-mile racecourse west of the railroad bridge. (SCRCTUL.)

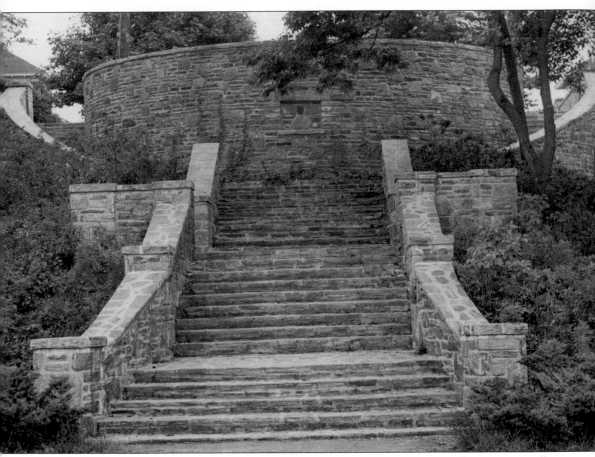

The WPA built three sets of Pennsylvania mica stonemasonry stairways with retaining walls in the late 1930s to connect the southern border of Cooper River Park with Collingswood. The largest staircase, shown here, descends from East Madison Avenue to South Park Drive. A pair of stonemasonry staircases with stone rails descend around the outside of the retaining wall and meet at a shared stone landing and descend to the park. (TUSCRC.)

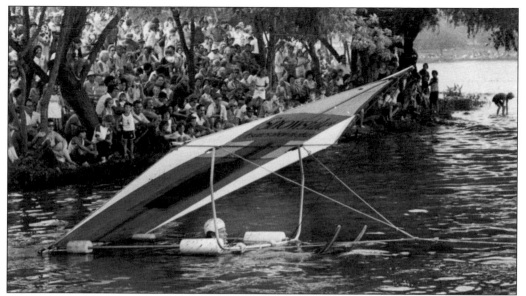

Spectators crowd the shore of Cooper River Lake in 1975 to watch a water-skier demonstrate kite sailing behind a motorboat. The first event, called "Flatkite" flying by Lynn Gilbert, was part of Camden County's Serendipity Sunday celebration. (SCRCTUL.)

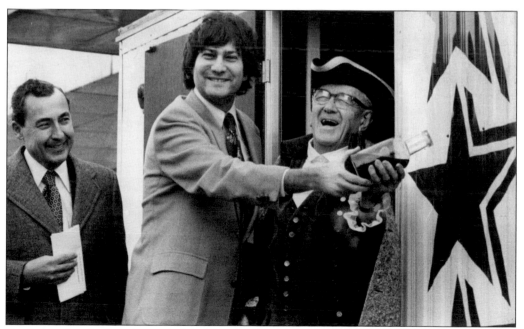

Freeholder Lewis Katz (center) christens the Camden County Historymobile in this February 1976 photograph. The water was gathered from the Cooper River and 14 other Camden County rivers and creeks and poured from an 1894 bottle used by the Joseph Campbell Co., predecessors of the Campbell Soup Company. Richard Hineline (left), president of the commission, and Harry Green, then New Jersey's oldest local government official and dressed in Colonial garb, assist. (SCRCTUL.)

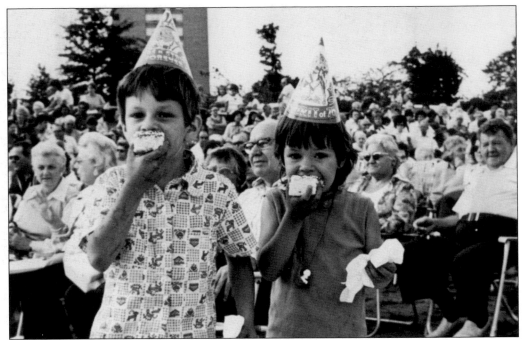

Two youngsters, Rocco and Gina Hagan, sample birthday cake on the north shore of Cooper River Lake in front of a crowd of seated spectators at Camden County Park's 50th-anniversary party in this July 28, 1976, photograph. (SCRCTUL.)

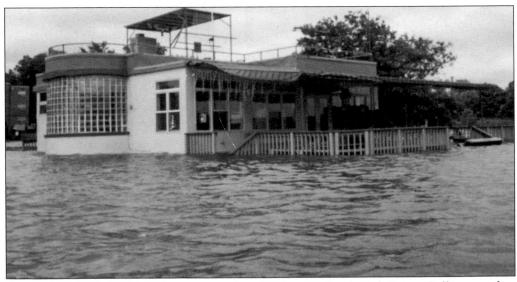

The Cooper River Yacht Club, constructed in 1945 at 450 South Park Drive, Collingswood, is surrounded by floodwater from the Cooper River in 2004. (CRYC.)

Since Hurricane Agnes caused breaches in the retaining banks between the Cooper River and Farnham Park's lake in the early 1970s, the Camden County Freeholders and Camden officials have ignored the lower portion of the park and allowed it to be exposed to daily tidal flooding. This has destroyed the park's historic recreation facilities surrounding the former lake, including the brick pavilion (pictured). A glaring example of "demolition by neglect," the pavilion caves in a little more each year, as tidal flows undermine its foundation and weather relentlessly deteriorates the walls, now that its roof has partially collapsed. The trash-laden shoreline and slumping pavilion are visual reminders of the failure of public officials to preserve and protect Camden County's historic resources. (SCRCTUL.)

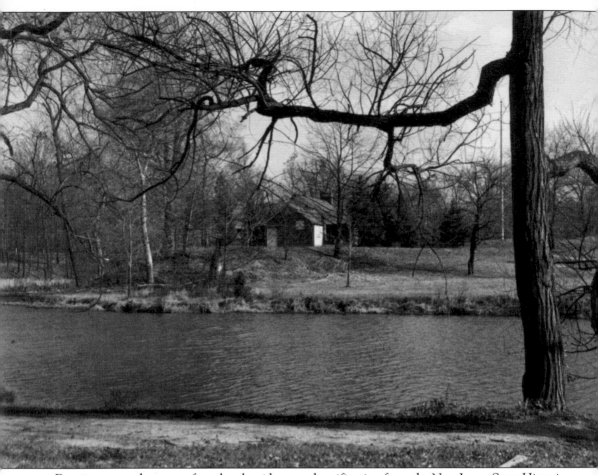

Despite repeated requests from local residents and verification from the New Jersey State Historic Preservation Office that the building qualified for protection as part of a pending application nominating the Cooper River Park Historic District to the New Jersey and National Registers of Historic Places, Camden County Park officials hastily demolished the Wallworth Park Clubhouse in March 2014. The 1928 clubhouse was the first building the Camden County Park Commission constructed. Designed to resemble a one-story brick Colonial building to be consistent with structures in Haddonfield's historic downtown district, the Wallworth Park Clubhouse commanded scenic views of Evans Pond and Wallworth Lake from high ground between Old Bortons Mill Road and Buckman's Run. (HPL.)

BIBLIOGRAPHY

Boyer, S. Charles. *Rambles Through Old Highways and Byways*. Camden, NJ: Camden County Historical Society, 1967.

Brown, C. Oscar, ed. *Camden County Park System as Constructed by Camden County Park Commission*. Camden, NJ: Camden County Park Commission, 1937.

Camden County Historical Society. *Historical Driving Tours of Camden County*. Camden, NJ: Camden County Historical Society, 1974–1976.

Camden County Planning Department. *Camden County Parks and Open Space Plan*. Camden, NJ: Camden County Board of Chosen Freeholders, 1972.

Clement, John. *Sketches of the First Emigrant Settlers Newton Township, Old Gloucester County, West New Jersey*. Camden, NJ: Sinnickson Chew, 1877.

Corotis, A. Charles and James M. O'Neill. *Camden County Centennial: 1844–1944*. Camden, NJ: Huntzinger Co., Inc., 1944.

Cranston, Paul F. *Camden County 1681–1931, Two Hundred and Fiftieth Anniversary: The Story of an Industrial Empire*. Camden, NJ: Camden County Chamber of Commerce, 1931.

Delaware Valley Regional Planning Commission. *A Teacher's Guide to the Watersheds of Camden County*. Philadelphia: Delaware Valley Regional Planning Commission, July 2003.

Delta Group. *Cooper River Study*. Camden, NJ: City of Camden, September 1980.

Dorwart, Jeffery M. *Camden County, New Jersey, The Making of a Metropolitan Community, 1626–2000*. New Brunswick, NJ: Rutgers University Press, 2001.

———. *Elizabeth Haddon Estaugh: 1680–1762, Building the Quaker Community of Haddonfield, New Jersey: 1701–1762*. Haddonfield, NJ: Historical Society of Haddonfield, 2013.

Dorwart, Jeffery M. and Philip E. Mackey. *Camden County, New Jersey, 1616–1976*. Camden, NJ: Camden County Cultural and Heritage Commission, 1976.

Fichter, H. Jack. *A History of Pennsauken Township*. Pennsauken, NJ: Pennsauken Historical Society. 1966.

Gillette, Howard, Jr. *Camden After the Fall: Decline and Renewal in a Post-Industrial City*. Philadelphia: University of Pennsylvania Press, 2005.

Hohmann, Heidi. "Charles Wellford Leavitt, Jr.," in *Pioneers of American Landscape Design*. Edited by Charles A. Birnbaum and Robin Karson. New York: McGraw-Hill, 2000.

Hopkins, G.M. *Atlas of Philadelphia and Environs*. Philadelphia: G.M. Hopkins, 1877.

Johnson, Eldridge. "Address: To the business men of Camden," supplement to *Health, Sunshine and Wealth*. Camden: Private publication, October 11, 1928.

Leavitt, Charles W., & Son. *Health, Sunshine and Wealth*. Camden, NJ: Eldridge Johnson private folio publication, undated. Distributed c. 1928.

Mathis, Mike. *Cherry Hill: New Jersey*. Charleston, SC: Arcadia Publishing, 1999.

Mathis, Mike and Lisa Mangiafico. *Cherry Hill: A Brief History*. Charleston, SC: The History Press, 2010.

Pennypacker, James Lane. *Verse and Prose of James Lane Pennypacker*. Haddonfield, NJ: The Historical Society of Haddonfield, 1936.

Prowell, George R. *The History of Camden New Jersey*. Philadelphia: L.J. Richards and Co., 1886.

Raible, Dennis G. *The First Three Hundred Years: Haddon Township's Hopkins Plantation*. Philadelphia: Saint Joseph's University Press, 1990.

———. *Down a Country Lane*. Camden, NJ: Camden County Historical Society, 1999.

Rauschenberger, Douglas B. and Katherine Mansfield Tassini. *Lost Haddonfield*. Haddonfield, NJ: The Historical Society of Haddonfield, 1999.

Schopp, Paul. "Sears, Roebuck and Company Retail Department Store Nomination, Camden City, Camden County, New Jersey." Washington, DC: National Register of Historic Places.

DISCOVER THOUSANDS OF LOCAL HISTORY BOOKS FEATURING MILLIONS OF VINTAGE IMAGES

Arcadia Publishing, the leading local history publisher in the United States, is committed to making history accessible and meaningful through publishing books that celebrate and preserve the heritage of America's people and places.

Find more books like this at
www.arcadiapublishing.com

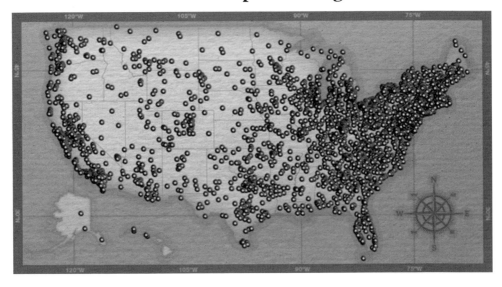

Search for your hometown history, your old stomping grounds, and even your favorite sports team.

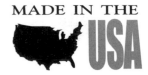